Cinderella Story

Bill Murray
with George Peper

Cinderella Story
My Life in Golf

Broadway Books

New York

BROADWAY

A hardcover edition of this book was originally published in 1999 by Doubleday, a division of Random House, Inc.

Broadway Books titles may be purchased for business or promotional use or for special sales. For information, please write to: Special Markets Department, Random House, Inc., 1540 Broadway, New York, NY 10036.

BROADWAY BOOKS and its logo, a letter B bisected on the diagonal, are trademarks of Broadway Books, a division of Random House, Inc.

Visit our website at www.broadwaybooks.com

First Broadway Books trade paperback edition published 2000.

Designed by Brian Mulligan

The Library of Congress Cataloging-in-Publication Data has cataloged the hardcover as:
Murray, Bill, 1950—
    Cinderella story: my life in golf / Bill Murray with George Peper. – 1st ed.
    p.   cm.
    1. Golf—United States Humor. 2. Murray, Bill, 1950– . 3. Celebrities—United States Biography. I. Title. II. Title: My life in golf
    GV967.B78 1999
    796.352´092---dc21   99-25300
    [B]   CIP

ISBN 0-7679-0522-9

00 01 02 03 04 10 9 8 7 6 5 4 3 2 1

Dear Reader,

This is what they in the business call a dedication page. That there is one at all shows some dedication and that the people still speaking to you are not just dedicated but devoted.

To my wife, Jennifer, and the boys, the holy noise between the silence. Thank God this period of our lives is over.

To my collaborator and friend, George Peper. George, please do it, pull up stakes and start a new life!

And Shawn Coyne at Doubleday, keep seeing the glass half-full, and it will dawn upon you that it's probably your turn to buy.

I didn't wish to write a book. It seemed any idiot could do it, and every idiot does. I tried not to pretend more knowledge than I have, but I got into trouble when I gave that up. You'll see where that happens. Also, it seems a publisher demands a certain number of pages and a certain number of words! Can you believe that? It sounds like punishment—for author and reader. Therefore, I apologize for pages 93 and 196–97. I wasn't allowed to go home until I finished.

I hope you enjoy the reading as much as I enjoyed the writing.

Keep in touch,
Bill

Cinderella Story

Monday

The light seems to come from everywhere. All of the trees, buildings, and cars seem as if they are lit from within. They rheostat down when the fog rolls in, and somewhere out there is the ocean, at any hour of the day, its breeze being flavored by one of the fireplaces in the hotel rooms of The Lodge at Pebble Beach. Yes, as a matter of fact, I *have* smelled Pebble.

There's no sound at this time of the morning, though there used to be before we went spikeless—another thing the peace movement wrought. I make out the rental car trunk through the haze. Now it's got a couple golf bags in it, and towels, umbrellas, and a few extra weather and fashion choices for the day ahead. Today's palette is central coast chameleon, nothing that would flush the fauna from the flora. Save the fine vines for later in the week, when they can serve to distract the gallery from my golf game.

At every intersection, every fork in the road, every parking lot, or every illegal-turn possibility stands a volunteer traffic marshal. And today, which way you wish to turn makes no difference. The marshals are calm. They haven't been drenched . . . yet. They meet your wave with a fearless smile. You can only tell them in the rearview mirror, "By the end of this week, you'll have lived through the first twenty minutes of *Saving Private Ryan.*

I am a contestant in the AT&T Pebble Beach National Pro-Am. It says so on the side of my car. And for one week, I'm on the Princess Cruise of amateur golf, playing the greatest stand of courses in pro golfdom in front of galleries larger than those at the Little League World Series at Williamsport, having more fun than I will have for the rest of the year. And it's only the first week in February.

That's the tough part. I live in the East, where February's golf also qualifies as curling. My challenge every year is to show up with my "K" game and triumph over a large field of the latest-technology, previously indicted, warm-climate sandbaggers.

And Monday at Pebble is the first day of the rest of your life, especially for someone who plays for keeps. This year would begin like the others. I knew I'd be playing in the Monterey Boys and Girls Club tourney at Monterey Peninsula Country Club. It's about the kids, of course, don't get me wrong, but it's also about getting the kinks out of the "K" game.

The AT&T used to be called the Crosby Clambake when Bing was in charge, but now that everything is sponsored by one corporation or another, it's called the AT&T Pebble Beach National Pro-Am. The free stuff you get when you register to play (phone calls and decanters) almost makes you forget that it's somewhat of a misnomer. Even though the final round is always played at Pebble Beach Golf Links, you have to shoot your way through the Poppy Hills Golf Course and Spyglass Hill Golf Course—as well as one early round at Pebble's links—before the promised land of a Sunday round for all of the marbles. Poppy and Spyglass are no day at the beach, and MPCC is the perfect tune-up round to get used to the ricochets of the woodland inland of Poppy and Spyglass, as well as the winds off the surf at Pebble. You have both kinds of holes going for you at MPCC. Which is nice.

On the way to MPCC, the 17-Mile Drive was transplendent. The sun was shining. The wind was thin. If the weather holds out—and it might—this could just be the year. Long ago, the roads between the golf courses were hewn by the railroad builders or the forty-niners, or the telegraph pole families (including women and children), or somebody. At night, they have the same charm

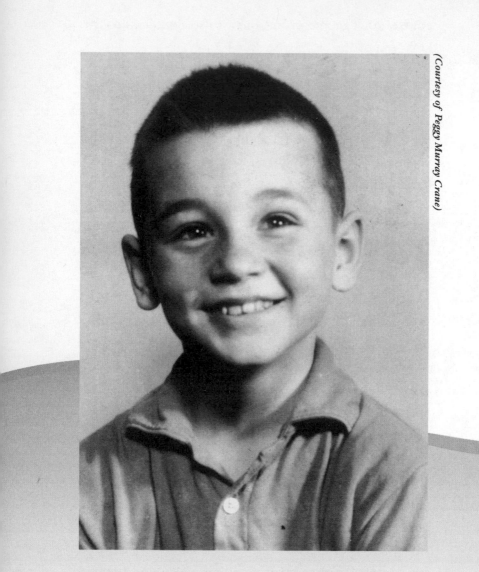

I wish I still had this shirt.

Bill and his brothers used to love caddying for Wallace Patterson, who was a lovely old guy but about 99 percent blind. He didn't play much—just the first hole and then seven, eight, and nine, but he'd sign a caddy card for eighteen holes. And since he couldn't see, they'd tell him where his ball went, or where they thought he'd like to hear it went. "Nice shot, Mr. Patterson," they'd say, to which he'd invariably reply, "Yes, I thought I'd caught that one pretty well." The ninth hole was a short par three that came back to the clubhouse. While in the care of the caddying Murray brothers, Old Pat made three holes in one, collecting a handsome trophy each time. Eventually the club caught on and told Bill and his brothers to knock it off.

—*Gordon Ewen,*
former President,
Western Golf Association

as those kindly German forests in the Grimm brothers' stories, the tale which ends with a little boy being eaten by a wolf. And with only the occasional wolf beheading by a friendly woodchopper, and the tyke freed from lupine digestion. Now, you see, you got me thinking about those forests, and those trees. And those Grimm brothers. What must the parents have been like? I must make sure to be out of the trees by nightfall. Those trees line the courses, too. Especially Spyglass and Poppy Hills. But we'll get to that.

Aw, why be a tease? Let's talk about trees. Here's a tight shot. Trees tight right, and a gentle tug to the left are more trees. A little too far away is a narrow green that slopes away, guarded by traps on both sides and back. What's wrong with this picture?

1. It's not Position A (golfer talk for the middle of the fairway); or,

2. I've used the word "trap" instead of "bunker."

Answer to come. Back to the business at hand.

One of the MPCC members, Bob Huntley, invited me to take part in this event a few years ago, and it has become my Monday. We play with Bill Brandt, a guy who makes this event go. There's no gallery, so Bill provides one: his daughter-in-law Susan, his grandson Steve, and his wife Patsy, whose job is to keep Bill in line. She quit her other job fifty years ago.

When you have the game, the looks, and the clothes, you
become that extraordinary creature, the supermodel.

Auric Goldfinger, at level par.

In *Quick Change* I played a clown who robbed a bank. That year Bill showed up and played in a full clown mask while doing lines from the movie. It's one thing to arrive at the tee in a mask. We've all done it. But to make the commitment to play the round masked; that's giving to the team. I remember my clown partner setting up, peering at the pin, and skittering a four-wood to the right. He looks at his divot and then mutters from beneath the mask, "That wasn't my best." A pastoral Pagliacci. Bill lost three pounds that round, and I kept the mask to use when venturing out of The Lodge. More important, when Bill heard about this book, he offered free use of a photograph of his dog, Cinderella. It was a gesture I'll never forget.

This is nice time, playing golf with a family of men and women who are comfortable in their own shoes, and with their game. I envy the nineteenth hole postscript: I've shot my age. So much so that I intend to live to a hundred and eight.

MPCC has exceptional success with this tournament for the Boys and Girls Club of Monterey. Success, my definition—a full turnout of pros and amateurs, a competitive field of evenly matched foursomes, good food and drink afterward, and last, an awards program that is short and fun, one that people stick around for. Michael Chapman achieved liftoff when he was MPCC's head pro.

The good name, charitable foundation, and considerable height of Davis Love Davis Love Davis Love put it into orbit. And members and the boosters have taken it from there. The fortuitous alignment of a PGA Tour event with a delicious golf course that foretells the terrain, feel, and challenges of the week to come at the AT&T tournament helps, too. There are charity events every week on the PGA Tour, but there aren't many like this one. Some are "celebrity" without celebrities, some are self-promotions by local shakers and movers, and some are forced-march autograph shows. Charity? Well, charity begins at home, but it never hurts to be too careful. Or so I once thought.

A BS detector is important in this age of telemarketing. But you can be wrong. I said you, not me, but in fact my favorite stories aren't about myself but on myself. It's a true pleasure to have your preconceptions about a person proven wrong. A pie in the face with no downside. Usually, we react to the seeing of our failures and weaknesses with more failure and weakness—shame, anger, self-justification, or self-pity. But when I'm wrong about someone and find out, it tickles me.

One day the phone rang, and a blustery fast-talking voice left rubber on my ear.

"Hi, this is Sterling Ball, out in California. Hope I'm not bothering you. I got your home number from your

On my way to a top-ten finish at the Roy Clark/Buck Owens Hee-Haw-aiian Open.

Scott Simpson, Cinderella Brandt, and me on a golf day when we were all dogs.

brother Ed. He said I should quit bothering him and bother you directly. You see, I'm putting together a golf tournament, and I could use a few celebrities. I figure if I can get you, it will make it easier to bag some more of you people."

(Uh-huh. Well, any friend of Ed's has got to be double-checked. My big brother is too tender, too delicate to be a good judge of character.)

"You're a friend of Ed's? Where do you know him from?"

"I'm not sure. I think it was playing golf. That's where I got the idea to ask you. To play. We got Eddie Van Halen to be our host."

(Okay . . . friend of Ed's, celebrity bagger, music-industry connections . . . that's three strikes with the bat on the shoulder.)

"What charity will benefit?"

"My own charity. The Casey Lee Ball Foundation. There's nothing set up yet, but any profit we make will go toward helping kids with kidney problems."

(This guy has got 'em. "My own charity!" Casey Lee Ball is an aunt who lives in a state without extradition. I bet Michigan or someplace.)

"Good. So the kids will get the profits, if there are any. Do you have any hopes of a profit?"

"Yeah, if I can keep the costs down. I don't belong to a golf club, so I had to rent a course, and they want a cash deposit . . ."

(Deep breath, very deep breath; don't ever let them hear you exhale.)

". . . so I laid out the twenty-five grand to cover it."

(I exhale low and slow, but somehow it catches in my throat!)

"But you've got people to feed, don't you? So . . ."

(He's heard me! Busted! By an amateur, a cold caller! But I had to find out this guy's angle. Naked now, I brace my back against the doorjamb.)

"So a friend of mine said he'd help me with the food. Oysters, crab legs, sushi. I put down some of my own money for prizes. I figure we can make some money selling tee sponsorships. Instead of a cardboard sign, I'll put the sponsor's name or company on a guitar neck that they can keep.

"I called to buy some airline tickets, and the guy from American got interested and donated some tickets and upgrade coupons. We're also going to limit the number of foursomes, so it won't be a five-hour round of golf. Maybe keep it to eighteen foursomes."

(It all sounds nice. Too nice. Seafood golf orgy nice.)

"Doesn't seem like there'll be too much left for your charity," I said.

"The goal is to raise eighty thousand dollars."

"Which doesn't sound like much. Not too ambitious."

"Just enough to cover the salary and cost to relocate a pediatric kidney specialist to the UCLA Medical Center. They could use one."

"How do *you* know that?"

"I got on the Internet trying to find one, and you'd think UCLA, the biggest, most prestigious hospital, with all its resources, would have one, but they don't; and they had no plans to get one, so I told them I'd get one. And so I've got a doctor willing to relocate. That way my son and I won't have to drive so damn much."

(The phone became terribly heavy; the voice seemed to come from very far away now.)

"When our son was diagnosed with kidney problems, we thought it was like any other illness—there's a medicine, there's a cure, someone somewhere knows all the answers, and Casey will be fine in a couple of weeks. That was just wishful thinking . . ."

(Casey. Casey Lee Ball. I wish I were anywhere else in the world right now . . . Even Michigan.)

"I guess this all became of so much interest to me when Casey needed a new kidney 'cause his weren't functioning well enough. I gave him one of mine. I wish I'd taken a little better care of it."

(I suddenly saw myself: five inches high, both arms over my head . . . holding a giant telephone. It was a long time before I could speak.)

At the UCLA Medical Center today, you can meet the relocated doctor. You can also visit the Casey Lee Ball Laboratory. And if you're really lucky, once in a blue moon, you might meet Casey Lee Ball.

I make it to MPCC just in time for tee off. The course is in as good a shape as I've seen it. Last year's El Niño beat up on these hallowed grounds, but word is that this year's winter has been pretty mild. It got up to the sixties today and even with a constant breeze on the back, the conditions were bearable. Word on the street is that rain is heading in for the weekend.

I had a hard time off the tee today, wasn't quite puring the irons the way I like to, and the short game left me short. So, you may ask, what keeps a man going when the chips are down? It's a journey, you animal, not a destination. You just keep plugging.

My father was a very difficult laugh. Adults found him very funny. But his children had a tough time cracking him up. One of my strongest childhood impressions is falling off of my chair at the dinner table while doing a Jimmy Cagney impression. I hit my head very hard on the metal foot of the table leg, and it hurt terribly. But when I saw my father laughing, I laughed while crying at the same time. I guess that was some kind of beginning.

My father, Edward, had nine kids: Edward; one year later, Brian; two years later, Nancy; two years after that, Peggy; one year later, Billy; two years later, Laura; four years later, Andrew; two years later, John; four years later, Joel. In those gaps were three children lost in pregnancy, including a set of twins. Rest in peace, little Murrays.

My mother, Lucille, bore the nine children, had those eleven pregnancies, and outlived my father by twenty-one years. Late in her life she told me that having babies into her middle age had kept her young.

As a young man, I thought that my father had been responsible for any sense of humor that I inherited and that it passed through him from my grandfather, who owned a bow tie that lit up, which he used very tastefully.

My siblings pointed out to me later, "You're just doing Mom."

This was so shocking all I could think was . . . "You mean my father was not my mother?"

Unless their father was a drunk or a brute, boys often don't think to take after their mother. Until it's too late.

Anyway, all of the kids ended up "doing Mom." There
are four of us who've tried show business. Five, if you
insist on counting my sister the nun, who does liturgical
dance. To date, she's the only one insisting that she's in
the business. I will include a liturgical dancer in show
business the day that one of them gets an encore . . .
the day that I hear . . .

"More! In the name of the Father, and of the Son,
more! We are not getting off of our knees until you come
on back out of the sacristy and give us just one more!"

The proof is, you could not be doing my Mom and be
doing liturgical dance. It's one or the other.

The moment of actual mother and child comic union
came only after Brian and I had made it in show business
to the tune of buying a new furnace for the house. This
somehow made us legit—and then some. She clutched
the entertainment industry to her success-breeding
breast as time warped, and life now jumped off the pages
of *Photoplay* magazine. She was an insider, a major Hollywood player, and an authority on all things entertainment. And like a player, very, very vulnerable.

The show business windfall had made possible a summer lake cottage rental, just over the Wisconsin state line.
I'd called her from New York.

"Sounds nice. Oh, nuts, that's probably too far to drive."

"What's too far to drive, Billy?"

"Well, it's up above Rhinelander. It's a place called the Showboat. It's a bit of a hump, but it is an incredible show to see. An amazing show. I guess you would probably call it a variety show? And they're all people who live up there, and they do the show up in the north woods. It's the only place I've ever seen them. I mean, this a show you would never see in New York. Ever. You have to go there to see it."

Well, Lucille bit like a spring muskie. I felt something on the line, and I thought it might be big. But it was a week before I reeled the whole story into the boat. Let me tell you about the show at the Showboat.

A beautiful horseshoe-shaped room, windows framing a gorgeous lake. Photos of the great Milwaukee Braves. An offstage voice introduces our emcee, who turns out to be the offstage voice. He bounces on, almost into your lap. The tables are that close to the stage. Unlike most of the men in the north woods, he wears high zippered patent leather boots, a green lamé jump suit, and a blond wig.

And we're off. He sings. He talks about how much he loves the fresh air up here, and about the Liberace memorial museum in his parents' home near Madison. Then . . . he brings on the other acts.

Joe and Rita Buck. "Ladies and Gentlemen, I give you Joe and Rita Buck." Most of the audience orders another draft. They are out for a long evening of entertainment. Joe sits and plays electric accordion. Rita stands, with the string bass. When they do a very slow and dramatic "Scarlet Ribbons," you could hear a tray drop.

Next there is a lady with a dog act, who cannot control the dogs—four of them. And you sit about six feet away from her as she struggles, using a stick and a whistle, to catch her dogs up to the recorded music.

A grandfather and son come up and play spoons. A fanfare brings up a bartender showing off the catch of the day. The largest fish pulled out of the lake today. A girl dressed in a sari dances to "Song of India." She exits to scant applause, and you see how tough it is for a liturgical dancer to make it.

Eventually, our emcee returns and thanks and pays tribute to an incredible man who had believed in him, shored him up against the monsters, taught him what love is. And given him someone to emulate. That man is here tonight, and would he stand, please?

Reverend James Something-or-other looked like guys who've been shot by a sniper—he looked alive, but you knew he was dead. There wasn't a walleye in the place as he jerked to full height and melted back into his chair.

No act could follow that, but the owner, Carl Marty, could. Checks were being settled as he took the stage with his Saint Bernard, Bernice. Carl may have been com-

With sister Peggy in 1951, wondering if Hogan could defend his Open title.

pletely bombed, I couldn't say for sure. (I didn't know
what "drunk" was until later on in life, the night my
friend John Thompson made me his Tom Collins and we
drove around Reno in a convertible VW bug.)

Uncertain as I was, Carl Marty did speak at length
while cigarette after cigarette ashed down his turtleneck.
He told the stories of Bernice's bravery in rescuing
injured woodland creatures—birds, squirrels, rabbits,
deer, and chipmunk. At his feet, unmoving, lay Bernice,
looking exhausted from her many sallies, or perhaps
dead. Nonetheless, incapable of getting Carl off the
stage. Finally, voices from the room began chiming in.

"You got that right, Carl."

"No, Carl, there aren't many animals unafraid of the
badger."

"God bless you, and may God bless Bernice."

"There'll never be another like her."

"Can we all go home now?"

It was Laura who finally told me what happened. She
was the only one Mom could get to go with her. They had
driven like madmen to get there.

"Billy said it was going to be a hump."

I love this vision of those two little women barreling
down roads simply called Highway X or Highway GG.
When night falls, guided only by the aurora borealis, driv-

ing deeper and deeper into the woods like Ahmet Erte-
gun looking for Robert Johnson.

They arrived just as it started. It took them about five
minutes.

"Billy, we had to drop our silverware on the floor so
we could hide our heads underneath the table."

"Oh, good, you found it. I wasn't sure you would."

At legal speed, it was a long ride back to the lake cottage. Plenty of time to absorb the show. Reflect. Fathom
the depth of family. And after, dispense a serving so that
all may be satisfied.

"How was the show?"

"Was it good? Describe."

"Astonishing. He didn't, it was . . . he really didn't
do it justice."

"He didn't. We really wished you had come. We
wanted to call, but there was a man who wouldn't get off
the pay phone."

"It was that good?"

"And tomorrow night is their last show."

"I would certainly want to go again."

"Is it sold out?"

No, as a matter of fact, it wouldn't be sold out. All of
those who failed to make last night's show would be able
to get seats close to the stage but not until after an incred-

ible hump. Once again, at speeds over ninety miles an hour, to arrive just in time for a breathless offstage voice to introduce our breathless emcee.

I'm not much of a practical joker. I'm afraid to be. Because although I can dish it out, I'm not sure I can take it. But it felt good to truly harpoon my mother. And she made me proud when she pulled the others under with her. There were more. And it was merrier. I had never seen her do that before, and it had to mean something. I think it meant now that I was finally an adult, she could finally act like a child.

So this is an up-by-the-bootstraps story of a boy who had Dr. King's dream: that one day a white man and a black man would walk hand in hand through the hills of Georgia. I have that dream. Or a version. Me and Ben Crenshaw's caddy, Carl Jackson, marching together through Amen Corner. Splitting the purse fifty-fifty. Just like Mr. Lincoln wanted it.

Which brings me back to home, "The Land of Lincoln," Illinois. Perhaps our nation's greatest state. She entered the Union in 1818. My hometown, Wilmette, was incorporated in 1847. The church I was baptized in was also founded in 1847.

Actually, I was born in Evanston. Uh-oh, it seems I've caught the "actually" virus. I meant to get the shot for it this year and forgot. This virus came out of the UK a few years back. Early symptoms include self-absorbed defensive anecdotes, crystallizing into terse, vacuous sentences, highlighted and usually beginning with the word "actually." It's lethal and can be contracted over the telephone.

"Is Mr. Merton in, please?"

"Actually, he's not."

"Might you tell me a good time to try back?"

"Actually, he's on a plane to Philadelphia right now."

"Good for him. Perhaps I'll try him the middle of next week . . ."

"Actually, he's coming back tonight."

"Oh, good. I'll try him tomorrow, then."

"Actually, he's not coming in tomorrow."

"'Actually,' could you put me on hold while I drive over there with some pepper spray and a dog muzzle?"

"Actually, I'm going home in about five minutes."

"Oh, I see. Okay, tomorrow for sure, then. Promise?"

There it is. You see what it is; you know what it is. All you can do is spray the phones with Lysol once a week.

So let's see. I was born . . . and learned golf . . . across the street.

We lived in a neighborhood of front lawns and side-walks, perfect for playing football, with the sidewalk and

(Courtesy of Michael Dann)

Find me.

the street serving as one out of bounds and the flower gardens and front porches the other. Each driveway was a first down, three driveways was a touchdown. We played tackle or touch if my sisters were playing. We tended to line up strong side left, the weak side out-of-bounds being oncoming traffic.

The Sisters of Christian Charity had their North American convent across the street, a giant plant with orchards, woods, a farm, graveyards, a carillon that played the Angelus three times a day, and tons of German nuns whose habits included a signature bow tie. They had no sidewalk on their side of the street, rather a perimeter fence punctuated by capped pillars. Each spring we chalked in these pillars with a baseball strike zone. The facades of the opposing houses were our outfield walls.

For golf, the grassy strip on the sisters' side of the street was our fairway. The telephone poles strung down the center of the strip, our pins. Pins and cups as well—if you hit the pole, you were in the hole. I remember a tense match between brothers, with Ed needing a fifteen-footer for the win. After looking at it for some time, building the appropriate tension, he took a full swing, hitting the pole about ten feet off the ground, the ball ricocheting high and far over our heads.

There were many ricochets to learn—off the fence into the fairway, off the fence into the convent, off a pillar into oncoming traffic, off oncoming traffic back onto the fairway, off the traffic, across the street, and into the bushes in front of the house and out of bounds . . . Creativity was required, and doggedness, too. Your opponent could miss from eight feet and you could hole out from forty yards over the convent fence. Talk about climbing back into a match!

So with the Murray family training regimen behind me, the narrow approach shot I'm facing—with trees left and right, the green sloping away, and traps lurking on both sides—doesn't bother me. (I told you we'd get back to course management. Pay attention.) I just need to decide whether to hit it straight or double-rail it off the trees on either side.

It should be in a chapter at the end of the book, on shotmaking, to be read after mastering my other techniques, but you seem to be coming along rather quickly, so let's continue. Often, after I've sought out a more pastoral, more private route from tee to green, my communion will be interrupted. That spooky pro partner of mine, Scott Simpson, that big lovable lug—thrifty, brave, clean, and reverent—is also a great tracker. When I ask how he finds me, he smiles and says, "I follow your spoor. Whatcha got, partner?"

"It's a caddy shot," I say, and he knows what I mean. Pros don't go to these spots on the course without a fiancée. The shot, if you can call it that, is so ridiculous as to be invented by a cruel challenger. But this is how we passed time in the caddy yard of my youth. I've been here in my mind's eye before and have little doubt I will again.

A caddy shot was a golf shot learned in the caddy yard. The yard was outside the caddyshack and hit the recreational trifecta by serving as football field and basketball court, too. And when we were still too young to do so inside the caddyshack, we learned to curse, smoke, and play cards for money in the bushes behind the ninth green. The rest of the time, we made a living.

My dough was going toward my education. I caddied to make enough money to pay my tuition to Loyola Academy, a Jesuit high school. This was a tradition among the hardworking Murray boys—a tradition that did not include Andy and John, who were gifted and lazy and attended public school with the heathens. It was those two who kept caddying from becoming the family business.

If you worked all summer, you'd make your tuition, and have a little money left over. That money would be gone by Thanksgiving. You'd then be broke until springtime, but your time was free and the sense that you had spent all summer working your way through school would be a memory.

It was quite an achievement to pay your way through school, and it felt great to tell folks that you had. But amassing the sum was slower than watching a cut heal. Three dollars and fifty cents per bag. Seven for doubles. Twenty-five cents if you were rained upon. Tipping was not permitted. I could not wait to get rich and start breaking that rule. Once I hit thirteen, I carried doubles. Before that, singles. Before that, I was a shag boy.

Here's the shag boy premise: Empty a bag of golf balls onto the practice tee, turn, and run for your life. Anxious-to-improve hackers would start their slashing when you were still thirty yards away with your back turned. They were usually new members who couldn't get a game until they reached the level of simply terrible. You tried to make a game of fielding them like a baseball outfielder. But baseball has three outfielders, doesn't it?

That stuff I didn't much like.

My brothers sort of paved the way. So by the time I got there, Ed (five years older) was already in the pro shop (he always wanted more) and Brian (four years) was the shoe guy.

Back then, we'd play matches using odd, old clubs, first pick getting a twenty-year-old niblick, fourth pick a Bobby Jones mashie. Eighteen-hole matches, the course charted by the winner of the previous hole. Behind bushes, around trees, over the caddyshack. The creative process, along with appropriate gamesmanship, taught you that you were never out of a hole. You could rally from anywhere, and a stymied shot was never daunting. It was dare-to-be-great golf. Seve wasn't Seve from tee to green.

Lou Janis was the caddy master. You had to get there by six-thirty to get a good loop. Louie didn't get there until seven, but if you were there waiting . . . He drove a Ford Falcon, although I don't think that was the car he saw himself driving. Always immaculately dressed—not in great clothes but very neat—the prince of polyester. He was just trying to beat it somehow, trying to get an edge. Louie was a gambler. He'd bet on anything— whether a member on the putting green would sink one or two of his three three-footer warm-up putts, whether or not a guy would pick up his tee after his opening drive, just about anything.

Louie had a scam he moved with the caddies, too. If you didn't go out, you had no money, but you still got hungry, so Louie let you charge against what you might make. He had everyone's charges up on the wall, and you'd pay them off after you got back in. Ed would go out twice but bring home only $12.80 because he bought something to eat. That was okay, but one day Brian came home with only $2.50. So at dinner the whole family grilled him.

"I had a hot dog and a Coke—that's eighty-five cents."

I've prepared for this.

The first year Bill came to our school, he had trouble learning to hit chip shots. He kept releasing the club, flipping his wrists in the follow-through. So Phil Rodgers used a gimmick reserved for only the direst cases. He took a 9-iron, placed the club shaft against the inside of Bill's left forearm, and wrapped it with athletic tape so that the club became a permanent extension of the arm. Immediately, Bill hit better chips, striking the ball with a crisp descending blow. Shortly thereafter we broke for lunch in the Grand Cypress clubhouse. Bill walked into the crowded dining room with the club still taped to his arm. He ordered a bowl of soup, which he ate with his right hand while carefully keeping his left arm vertical with the club pointed to the sky. To all in the restaurant, this was a hilarious sight. To Bill, it was just life as usual.

—*Kevin McKinney,*
Director,
Academy of Golf at Grand Cypress

"And then what?"

"And then I had an ice cream sandwich."

"That's fifteen cents. You're still missing $4.50 . . ."

He was really sweating. In the end, it became known that Brian was smoking cigarettes, had bought some, and was trying to lie about it. He was about fifteen at the time.

B caddies would loop for Louie on Mondays—really so he had someone to take his bag when he wanted to play—so he could point out mistakes you made that were keeping you from seniority. Once you were a made man, you caddied for him when he played with his friends. All the area caddy masters played $5 skins with "umbrellas," a combo game with a point for prox, a point for low ball, and a point for low two-man team total. With birdies, everything doubled. I looped for him a few times—also helped him pick college football teams. Back then he knew me as "New Murray."

So these days, when the chips are down and my ball's in trouble and my opponent is tittering, I think back to the caddy yard of my youth. I actually relax when I see a so-difficult shot that requires Shakti visualization. I prefer it. To me, the scariest words in all of golf are, "It's a straight putt."

Tuesday

Our foursome came in third yesterday, anchored by PGA Tour pro Chris Couch. Anchored rather than led. He had an off day and didn't help us much. However, Chris did contribute by depressing us—his drives consistently landed about 290 off the tee. But he's as easy to be with as a guy who hits it that far can be.

Now the PGA Tour. We can talk about them, 'cause it's early in the week and they're not all around us yet. And among those who love the game, the Tour is a sect to be watched. At this tournament, they're camped right down the road, like tinkers. So lock your doors and count your clubs when you finish your round.

Come on, more bad stuff.

Okay. They whine about how hard the courses are and about how hard golf is. They won't play if it gets too wet, yet think nothing of what fourteen 90-degree-heat holes in khaki trousers and quite obviously briefs will look like to TV viewers. Betel-nut-chewing Indonesian paddy workers are more body conscious. As a group they own more pairs of white shoes and saddle shoes than a Junior Nationals Cheerleading Contest. The clothes they wear are given to them. They are paid to wear them. Well, there's not enough money in the world . . . Ugly, of course, is in the eye of the beholder. But can't their clothes at least come with instructions for coordination?

The PGA Tour events themselves, though, have an organization that would make the Cosa Nostra jealous. Say what you will about Deane Beman—I won't interrupt—but he created a steamroller that runs like Patton's Third Army. At every stop, hundreds of volunteers of all age groups work for the love of the game and to say thanks for the Wednesday Pro-Am that benefits their local charities. An absolutely brilliant stroke. Over a year, it is an enormous amount of money, which makes the enormous purses more than jake.

When the circus leaves town, it's truly missed, and folks look forward to next year's return. That's more than I can say for some of the movie crews I've been a part of. There is respect for the local environment. They say thanks, they recycle, they put on an exhibition, sometimes even a show. Golf is perhaps the only professional sport that realizes a gravy train with biscuit wheels

Thanks for the ruling. Room 204. It'll be just us.

shouldn't leave ruts. They actually act like contributing members of society.

And my own golf? The finest of my life, three days before the tournament begins. Slip these moccasins on, please.

"How are you hitting 'em, Bill?"

"I'm playing the best golf of my life."

How do they feel? Not too tight? Just continue walking in them for another 1,755 yards.

It's like being drunk, in that it's heady; but even the most complex California cab never made me feel this way. My golf must be affecting my state, as I wasn't aware that my state was affecting my golf. This may be so shallow it hurts, but hey, this is a book, not a relationship. Fasten your seat belts, it's going to be a lumpy ride.

For your consideration, this lightning bolt: Good golf breeds good behavior. In *Golf in the Kingdom*, Michael Murphy presented what may have been a blueprint for good behavior. Or not. But even the suggestion that the discipline of the game demands attention to task, denial of impure impulses, or the reunion of mind and body—a reunion more important than high school or Martin and Lewis—leaves most golfers puzzled after a round, like "Where did I leave my car keys?" This kind of reunion in today's world can really throw you.

At MPCC yesterday, I got a taste of direct experience. My 220-yard uphill rocket left a tap-in par at eighteen . . . Okay. Mind and body perfectly in sync. Then follow, in order: inability to find caddy, golf clubs, or automobile; with no street shoes, and locker room attendant gone, appearance at after-fest in dried-mud spikeless, two-toned Gore-Tex Etonics; extremely civil, extremely long line at bar; wrong guess on "white or red"; third place on a card-off; children not my own asking questions I can't answer; bummed ride home in a shared bucket seat with adolescent possessing six knees and eleven elbows; consequent lockout of my room and round trip to the front desk for an extra key.

And how do you explain a later report that someone thought they'd seen me walking to my room with Abraham, Martin, and John? After a mother/child, mind/body reunion, it can all begin with "Where did I leave my keys?" Well, perhaps the words of a golf widow (name withheld upon request) will touch a heart probably hardened by years of incorrect sprinkler yardage.

"He can be nice after, sure. If he's birdied eighteen. Once he chipped in to win the back, the press, and the overall; so he took me and the kids out for dinner. That was nice. And then one night he called from the car phone, slurring a bit. He'd eagled fifteen, he was coming home, and he meant business. 'Brace yourself, Bridget. Your master's on his way.' And he hung up.

I was a year ahead of Bill in high school, but I remember him as a kid who liked to sit and observe people in the hallways. He'd select a spot where he could avoid the wrath of the Jesuit priests for loitering, then just sit and take it all in. If someone stared back at him, he just made a face at them, a consummate goof-off. Back then we used to say Bill Murray was the man least likely to succeed. Guess we called that putt a little early.

—Michael Dann,
Assistant Director,
Carolinas Golf Association

Yep. Tied it myself.

"First thing, he sends the kids to play next door. Then he rushes me. It was kind of uncomfortable at first—he was talking in tongues, I think. Then he roared, really loud, fell back, and fainted. But for a few minutes he'd felt like he used to, and I was excited to be with him."

Not Tammy Wynette, but a witness. For the defense. Good golf/good behavior? You make the call.

Among the titans of industry playing on the practice range with me this week are many Horatio Alger stories and many equally touching inheritance stories. My own rise to the playing surface came after a scrambling front nine that opened with childhood disappointment.

For a serious grade school performer, there's only one part in the Christmas play. The Virgin Mary is a laydown for the fairer sex—Donna Reed, Olivia de Havilland, "ladies and gentlemen, Miss Meryl Streep." The nuns would choose a girl with excellent church-kneeling posture. And not one of the pretty girls in class, either—we don't want to send *that* message.

The role of baby Jesus? If not portrayed by a Betsy Wetsy, this part goes to the pupil who hasn't had a significant growth spurt since delivery. And that leaves the daddy of all roles: Joseph. The complexity, the layers . . . "Don't cry, little tower of ivory, we'll just get married." How secure was this guy? Unfazed by Nazarene gossip . . .

Notre Dame in the kitchen, putting her spin on lentil soup
. . . *The Word* incarnate playing on the floor . . .

"Jesus, Jesus, this is the most beautiful finger painting
I've ever seen! I'm going to hang it over my workbench!"

As you can see, I'd done the prep work and was ready
to apply two coats. But it was over in a second. I wasn't
even considered for Joseph, and I came back to my senses
in a cattle-call audition for the innkeeper.

I rally. Hey, it's a bad-guy part and you can score with
those. But not just bad . . . complex. I think it through:

"No reservation at the holidays?" Slam door . . . a
beat . . . reopen. "Say, those contractions of yours, just
how far apart are they?"

Dickensian. A foreshadowing of my work in 1988's
Scrooged, which should have been good 'cause I already
did the innkeeper, regionally, at St. Joseph's grade school
in Wilmette, Illinois.

Excuse me? Matt Klein? The innkeeper will be played
by Matt Klein? Tailspin. Free fall. Rapid substance abuse
(chocolate milk), withdrawal, followed by a pint-sized
James Mason walking into the ocean. (Remember *A Star Is
Born*? The second one . . . Do I have to spell them all
out for you?) I end up on a riser, with all the other no-
talents, singing carols between acts.

I talked through the entire show. ("The story was good,
but I wasn't grabbed: The actors didn't make me care.")

The sight of me motor-mouthing—too many rows up for her to get me with her combination knuckle-and-Bride-of-Jesus-wedding-band noogie—sent Sister Ivania practically Pentecostal. Jelly don't shake like that. The very sight of me in the yellow cardboard halo of the "riser people," disrupting the cherubs and seraphs. Well . . .

Ah, the joys of a child. Dogs, trees, leaves. Watching schoolteachers lose it so bad they have to be restrained by other teachers. And when that teacher is cowling, muttering, and dressed in black from head to toe, including a black veil, there exists the long-shot possibility she may just melt into a lovely little Margaret Hamilton puddle (Remember *The Wizard Of Oz?* Could these references get any easier?), leaving us her habit and rosary to play dress-up.

They say in my biz, you meet the same people on the way down as on the way up. Maybe, but I don't think Ivania's still in the trade. Call it mean reunion talk, but I heard she'd offered to direct *The Loaves and Fishes* in exchange for her eternal soul, and the producer turned her down.

Charity, as my mother used to say, charity. How about a little charity.

Well, the next time this happened . . . what, you think I went directly to the 1984 National Association of Theater Owners Star of the Year? No. See, that's the myth. It's a struggle.

Andy. Dad. Laura. Mom. Pat Boone.

Larry Basil.
The Music Man.

Mr. Bartosz with his game face on.

We were going to do *The Music Man* at Loyola (the caddy money repository). Well, the music man, Professor Harold Hill—again, the complexity, the layers—it's *type-casting*, right? And I'm a ringer for Robert Preston. Dead ringer.

Larry Basil got the part of Professor Harold Hill. And I forgave Larry, just as I recently forgave Matt Klein. Larry had talent, he could play about any instrument he could lift. He was a musical man, anyway. But your boy here gets his first real-world lesson: It's who you know.

Kenneth Bartosz, who had come to Loyola with the mandate to form a band, was the codirector of the play, it being a musical. With countless hours in musical rehearsal required, K.B. had final-cut casting approval.

So is it I, whose body language sang disdain for the fight song that Bartosz had written and urged us to sing in the gym at pep rallies with our schoolmates and at football games in front of girls in skirts and scarves? Oooorrrrrrr . . . Larry Basil? The centerpiece of the fledgling band, an actual musician in a high school of perfect-toothed boys, Basil led the band when Bartosz fumbled with sheet music or used the rest room. And Basil had also appeared at the head of the band the day it morphed into a marching band—though technically a standing band—led them onto the field of glory, knees high, beefeater hat atop his head, whistle in his mouth,

Texas-sized baton in his hand, in a maroon and gold-button-festooned drum major's outfit. An all-boys' school, sixteen hundred students, one guy out there leading perhaps a nineteen-piece band, standing in the Grambling University drum major's vines. Talk about a secure guy. Now I'm thinking Bartosz had one of those outfits himself in the closet and had a soft spot for a guy like Larry.

When you don't get Harold Hill, the bump-down is the barbershop quartet. But you forgot that "barbershop" rhymes with Bartosz, doesn't it? I think you may be starting to appreciate the struggle I was talking about. This is the moment, a biographer's moment: Jim Thorpe at Carlisle . . . Washington at Valley Forge . . . Hasselhoff in *Knight Rider*.

Then suddenly a grace from above. I did not have jug that day of auditions. (Jug from the Latin word for yoke. Jesuit irony/commentary. I should have been Latin for "the rack.") All the screwheads ended up in jug. But everybody got jug sometime. For the rare bird, it was the ghost of Christmas future.

"I don't belong here with these screwheads! Where are we?"

"Lompoc Federal minimum-security lockup for white-collar criminals."

A prefect would give each lucky attendee his yoke: a page ripped from a pocket dictionary. To be memorized.

You'd usually be asked three words. If you answered
them correctly, you went free. So while the straights and
those who'd been framed did their "Why am I here with
the animals?" meditation, a lifer could scan the defini-
tions for words that appeal to the cruelly comic bones of
a Jesuit. So when the official jailer for the day came in,
not knowing yesterday's inmates from today's, there was a
shot at a miraculous coop fly.

The key: Be all business, wanting out. When a kid
lipped off, shake your head in condemnation, and when
the jebby pimped somebody, smile in grateful appreciation of belated justice. Stand up to recite before it was
your turn, realize your error, and sit back down. Your
anxxxxxxiousness to go and your apparent knowledge of
your page duly noted, you could then let other guys go
before you while you actually studied. Then a grand angry
face, signifying that you'd been cut in front of, would earn
you a further stay of testing. As with crossword puzzles,
there are tricks to the doing that the great ones master.
Until finally.

"Get out here, Murray . . . 'Protozoan.'"

"Protozoan, protozoan, oh, okay. Protozoan, any of
the single-celled microscopic organisms belonging to a
type, er, to a group that includes the most primitive
forms of animal life."

"That would be you, Murray. Get out of here."

Back when Bill was a caddy at the Indian Hill Club, I was a waitress. I remember him as a cute boy and so funny—you never knew what he'd say next. But I can recall one moment as if it was yesterday. Bill was walking toward me, across the clubhouse lawn, with a set of golf clubs on his shoulder. When he reached me, all he said was "Nellie, you're going to see me someday in Hollywood."

—Nellie Kerrigan,
Clubhouse Manager,
Indian Hill Country Club

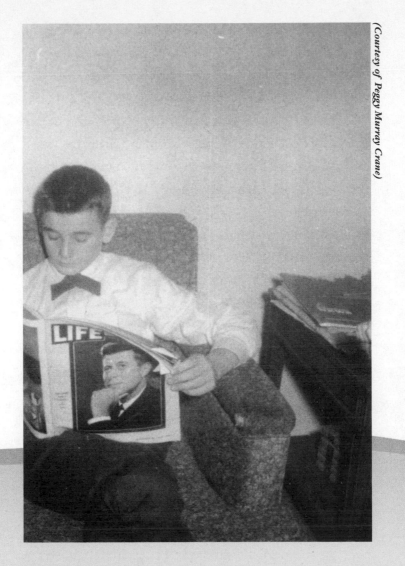

Big footsteps.

"What a feeling. I think I may just go out and sin no more. Let these halls be my runway to the rest of the world. I certainly don't belong in there with those animals."

But what . . . what is that noise? It piccolos out into the empty halls, and I peek into the little theater it emanates from. I'm going to look up "emanate" from the Latin (*e*, out + *manare*, to flow). To come forth, issue, as from a source.

That sound, oh, that sound? Girls' voices. Bouncing, laughing girls' voices in what seconds ago was a male prison.

"What is your name?" said a pretty, athletic woman.

"Papillon . . . Murray. Bill Murray."

"Okay, jump up in the back row and try to follow what the ones in the front are doing."

The ones in the front were girls, and they were moving in perfect unison with a girl's body—something I'd been considering doing for quite some time, even as a possible career.

Improbably, the dancers' tryout for *The Music Man* seemed even shorter than my innkeeper audition. I didn't know what it meant when a choreographer chose me to be in the troupe. Until she said, "I teach in the day, so our rehearsals will all be at night."

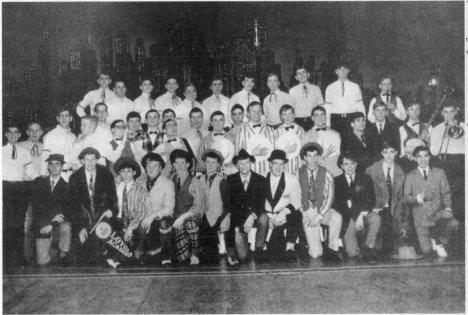

The cast of *The Music Man*.

I see. Because you teach in the daylight, I will be required to leave the comfort of my home immediately after dinner. The home I share with five brothers and three sisters. Leave that home on a school night and rehearse with the girls until eleven-thirty. I think I understand now. As Gandhi said to the Hindu who had killed a Muslim, "I know a way out of hell."

Yeah, and out of the ghetto, too, Mohandas. Showfolk work nights. They get breaks on homework, too, showfolk. Showfolk don't have school nights but rather nights when rehearsals end early and the time till eleven-thirty is filled riding in your co-trouper's daddy's Cadillac, drinking stolen gin out of eight-ounce 7-Up bottles.

This may not be the inspirational read that Moss Hart's *Act One* was for me, but I say unto you, Alleluia, Alleluia, there are many paths to the top of the mountain, Alleluia.

God damn it. When does he get to the golf lesson!!!? This *is* the golf lesson, animal. This kind of parable in personal growth must surely have an echo in every golfer's life. In so many cases I can think of, the simple miracle of employment is enough confidence builder for a downhill, sidehill six-footer! #1. Look at the line of the putt. #2. I have a job I do well enough to get paid. #3. Knock it in the damn hole, boss. That's enough to work on for now.

Wednesday

It's Wednesday morning, a good morning to sleep in, but since it's the last quiet morning before the tournament, the feel-good move is early breakfast at The Gallery coffee shop. Dee Keaton will be there, and the Hershiser brothers, a good test of whether I have sufficient humor to make it through the week.

Dee's okay, I can get a chuckle out of him—no big laughs, but the chuckle. He also will chuckle if you're trying to make him laugh; you know, a little something for the effort. An older wealthy woman will do a nice thing when she sees you are trying to make her laugh. First she'll stare at you, then her eyes go out of focus as she chuckles the words, "Oh, you're being funny." The chuckle ends abruptly with the second syllable of "funny"; she will turn and walk away. The French, I remember, will drift off your gaze and matter-of-factly say to the person next to them, "*Il fait une pleasantrie.*"

Which brings us to Orel Hershiser, baseball player, nicknamed "Bulldog." His neck, shoulders, and jaw stiffen as he fights any impulse to laugh. I guess it must be good for his rotator cuff. His brother Jud, the decent one, will laugh both at the pleasantries and his brother's apelike upper body tension. Jud must take after their mother, because the unlaughing father, Anel, sits there working on his rotation, too.

It isn't important to me that Hershiser laughs. I'm in it for the juice, the comic plyometrics of repeatedly bouncing off his solar plexus. Orel can be had, though, and it is delightful. See, he is a circus-clown quality giggler. Which is one of my favorite predilections. The one time I got him good we were talking about pygmies. This guy is six foot six, and anybody under three and a half feet tall just slays him. He may still bleed Dodger blue, but the truth is, pygmies can make him wet.

The Gallery's floor-to-ceiling windows overlook the first tee, the putting green, and the main entrance to The Lodge. Lots to see and comment upon, before you get to the weather. I need to know who this year's sandbaggers will be, and Dee will know, because Dee knows all things. After all, he won this Pro-Am a couple of decades ago. He had some help from Hale Irwin, but that was long before Hale jumped on the anabolic steroid bandwagon.

Now we know past champion Andy Garcia will never receive eighteen shots again and there will be no red flags like the eleven handicapper who shot 73 at Cypress Point on a Tuesday. Or Mr. Matshi Yamata, who won the team trophy with a fifteen handicap. (His course in Japan had been called to check his handicap; it turned out his course was *his course*.) And still no re-entry from Kerry Packer, the megalomaniac twenty-handicap Aussie who teamed with Greg Norman to finish forty-two under par. Greg, at four under par for seventy-two holes, did not play to his handicap. Packer didn't exactly help the team thirty-eight shots; they just ham-and-egged it really, really well.

By eleven o'clock the grounds will be packed for the celebrity shoot-out, which is usually fun; but there are always those complainers who come all the way out and are disappointed when there isn't a big pile of dead celebrities full of bullet holes.

Ex-Mayor Eastwood, Jack Lemmon, Tom Smothers, and Glen Campbell are regulars, supplemented by actors who've had enough time off to take lessons: Costner, Garcia, Quaid, that horrible Joe Pesci. Sometimes there are six or seven, sometimes a dozen or more. Sometimes the format is total score over the five-hole layout (one, two, three, then seventeen and eighteen), sometimes elimination.

The Northern California Golf Writers' Dinner; cheating death, with Bob Murphy and a wicked stepsister, prom queen Scott Simpson.

I was chairman of a major event at our country club, and somehow convinced fellow member Bill to be our after-dinner entertainment. Little did I know that this was a huge thing for him to agree to. Despite being one of the world's funniest men, Bill absolutely hates doing stand-up comedy. He agonizes over it. "It's only thirty minutes," I told him, to which he replied, "I don't think you know just how long thirty minutes is." I thought nothing of that remark until it came time for him to perform. He called me up to the stage and asked me to sit in a chair next to the podium. Then he invited a man from the audience to join us. The fellow turned out to be a local cop who produced a set of handcuffs. Bill then pulled my arms around my back and cuffed me to the chair, where I sat facing the audience throughout his entire, hilarious *forty-five*-minute performance.

—*Dan Zucchi,*
Sleepy Hollow Country Club

If my folks could see me now, sharing the bill with Dirty Harry.

One year I made it to the final hole, just me and John Denver. I wasn't intimidated by his bangs or his high voice. Or his illegal clubs, or the steroids he was obviously abusing. Hey, it was his choice. He had a sizable putt on eighteen to win. I'd had personal problems that year, and just as he was taking it back, I asked the crowd to thank him for the songs he'd given us. Well, God bless that crowd, they gave him a nice standing ovation.

John was polite enough, but soon he again wanted to putt. But before he could, I reminded those folks of some of John's lesser-known songs, songs covered by other artists, and songs we've all grown to know and love. Well, God bless that crowd if they didn't find some pretty sweet high harmonies before giving John another richly deserved standing ovation.

Damned if the Rocky Mountain sonofabitch doesn't knock in the twenty-footer.

It was worth it. I had a hootenanny full of fun. And J.D. had the peak athletic moment of his too-short life. He said, if I ever wanted to stay in his guest house in Aspen, I'd be welcome. Be warned, out there, I will show; just to tell this story again, and maybe have a look at his view.

Golf at its most insidious is golf as sales tool. The courtesies and niceties of the game can be elevated to paint the seller in a totally inaccurate, flattering light.

Chatter, which in a sales-pitch meeting would be easily disregarded as a campaign speech or other drunk talk, somehow gets in between the ribs, just by the element of surprise.

"God Almighty, that was a great shot!", when spoken with admiration and with an added soupçon of "I could never hit a shot that good" can fool just about anybody.

It's the simplest of bump-and-runs. You use it when you've got a lot of ego to work with. You want to land it just on, and let it roll right up to the one-way mirror.

"I know this guy's trying to sell me something, but I think my seven-wood just told him who's calling the shots."

The great ones, adding just a pinch of resentment, can convincingly infer that their Advil has been laved with sodium pentothol: "I never realized how muscular you are! You're a horse! Look at the calves on this guy!"

Wives, beware. If your man's not getting enough stroking at home, some sales floozy who knows how a man needs to feel can come along and ruin your happy home.

I don't know how the hell some of them sleep at night. It's the lies unlike any other that delight me. There is one that lives in my head like Lou Gehrig's farewell.

The buyer has just hatcheted a putt from twenty feet away: a five-hopper with backspin that forces the ball to check up about four feet short. The stunned silence is shattered by a booming, resigned, "Take that away."

Yes, please! Take that away! Anybody who can leave a ballmark when he putts should head to the next tee.

The acceptee walks away, performing a pelvic stretch usually associated with a nerveless setting down of a crippled RCAF bomber atop a Swiss glacier.

These same kindnesses of golf can also be used to serve mankind, to improve the condition. A traffic cop who lets you off with a warning isn't failing to uphold the law. Conceding a missable putt, or very missable, as we say, may not be cheating. Golf is megadoses of humility. It's not intended to break people. It shouldn't be about tears.

I play by the Rules. I call penalties on myself. Golf rules are fun to keep, but the living is sometimes more important than the game, and compassion is required. This is something no one talks about, that there are times the Rules aren't broken but suspended. Certainly not in competition, or any time to your golfing advantage, but where life would get stranger than necessary.

When your playing partner has just taken a deep breath and asked, "Do you think my marriage is a sham?" You may have just given up searching for a lost ball, but this is not the time to return to the tee to play a provisional. Sure, you could still make bogey. You could also birdie in with an eagle at the last. Please don't. Don't become one of them. Drop a ball and finish the hole. Take the maximum allowed for your handicap, triple bogey, quad.

If you can show compassion enough to give a putt to a suffering golfer, can't you show the same compassion and take a nine for yourself? Of course, later, when you're going over your round with the missus and she sees eights and nines, you've got to be prepared for "Honey, you had forty-one on the front, fifty-seven on the back with four nines. Are George and Libby Peper having trouble with their marriage?"

Anyway, the shoot-out format is fun but can be tricky to pull off. The rules change. Carryovers confuse things; putt-offs can be off-putting. There can be so many contestants, the gallery can't see what's going on. Ditto TV crews. Some don't understand that the people standing behind them are not watching television. It's distressing to see video claim eminent domain over galleries that have marched eighteen holes. Same old story: The grunts do most of the work; the flyboys get the glory.

My favorite shoot-out took place in 1988 at Butler National, site of the Western Open. My friend Bubba Phillips's brother Bobby's friend Tommy Fitzgerald's brother Brian was how I got there.

They made it fun. The shootout involved six pros: Peter Jacobsen, Mark McCumber, Larry Nelson, Scott Verplank, D. A. Weibring, and a loser by the name of Scott Simpson. They were all losers in my mind then, compared to the amateur lineup. It was, well, me . . . and Ernie Banks of the Cubs, Doug Wilson of the Black Hawks, Mike Ditka of Da Bears, Walter "Sweetness" Payton also of the Football Hall of Fame, and Michael Jordan of the Bulls. Not an actor in the bunch. All of us just great athletes.

How Bubba's brother's friend's brother got all these guys, I don't know; but the crowd at the first tee was both delirious and deranged. The drives alone were worth the excursion to the boondocks. The six pros hit it far and sure. Impressive. Hell, it's very impressive to see six pros tee off one after the other. It's not like most foursomes where, after a bad drive, you can toss out, "Okay, I got my guy."

Then came the choppers. If you can call guys choppers whose collection of jewelry included Super Bowl rings, Most Valuable Player ID headbands, Home Run Champion scarab amulets, Division Championship false teeth, and Actors' Equity medic alert bracelets.

These tee shots were not hit as straight as the pros' were. Yet they were not crooked or wild. They were all tagged, and they were all awe-inspiring, like fireworks. Each had a loud, frightening report, a magnificent, breathtaking trajectory, and enough *oohs* and *aahs* to make Siegfried and Roy giddy with happy silly.

This was not Gene Sarazen leading off the Masters, folks. This was a show of force. Forget distance, these balls were punished. With wood. When the career rushing leader wishes to make an emphatic point, count yourself lucky if you've got a white head that's square. And unless you want what Juan Marichal's slider got that night at Candlestick against the wind, stay off the tee! Women and children first!

Maybe you want to go one-on-one with the swing plane finish of a six-foot-six-inch harrier jet whose pleasant dreams involve the breaking of defenders' wrists on the rim; then by all means, don't bother staying behind the ropes.

Or perhaps your manhood says you gots to have a throw-down with any dude be sporting a positron-accelerator backpack and ain't afraid to use it on no eleven-story marshmallow figure; then you just bring it on, homey, just bring it on!

I kid. But I did kill my drive. Wounded it, anyway. I was jacked, Jack. My aortae were dispensing pharmaceutical adrenaline.

All my friends from high school were there; my cousins, brothers, and sisters were there; my mother, dying of cancer, was there. The heroes of my youth, adolescence, and extended adolescence were all there. At that moment, only Davis Love and his rainbow could have given me a fight. I looked up in that Illinois sky and thought I saw, you guessed it, the railsplitter himself, Abraham Lincoln, looking down on me and smiling. I, too, from humble beginnings had achieved greatness. I had gotten off the first tee with respect. Naturally, I did not hit another decent shot for quite a while.

The last to hit was Doug Wilson of the Black Hawks. By this time, the crowd and players had already been splashed with shards of balata. But Wilson hit a one-timer, a shot that no one who witnessed it could forget. Unless they repressed it for self-preservation reasons. This rocket went past my ball. And Walter's, Ditka's, Banks's, Mike's, and all of the pros', down about 300 yards. And there, where no one had really thought about it, or noticed, the hole began to dogleg. And Doug's ball just signaled, turned left, and went around the corner. The professionals got quiet in a big-eyed way. It was a fitting finale to the fireworks. And everybody lied/lay just one.

Peter Jacobsen, golf rocker, was my partner, and thank God. He was playing great that week. In fact, with my help, after three rounds of the tournament he led by four strokes. But I had marching orders to drive my sons to northern Wisconsin. There was a water-skiing tutorial that we felt the boys would need in order to get into an Ivy League school. It was Peter's responsibility to win the tournament without me. By himself, as it were. I thought it would be very good training for him.

Way up north in the land of cheese and mosquitoes, it was difficult to find the golf broadcast. There was only one television station, and no cable.

"Hi! You're the new people! Hello!"

"Hello. Marge, there's some people here . . ."

"We're from next door. I'm the son-in-law, and this is my brother, and these are my two sons. What happened to the Baumanns?"

"Well, Elmer didn't think he could keep up the place, so they decided to sell and move back to Cedarburg. That's where they came from . . ."

"Well, nice to meet you. I see you have a satellite dish on the lawn. What are you watching?"

". . . Then he died, you know, and so then she had the place and a sister down there in Cedarburg. The children were his, you know."

"What are you watching?"

"Drake, what are we watching?"

"I don't know."

"Are you watching ABC?"

"Why would I? What's on ABC?"

It's not sweat, folks. It's blood.

"The golf."

"The golf?"

"Are you watching the golf? The PGA Tour. The Western Open, down in Chicago. They're playing the final round right now. Look at the size of this remote. This is great. Does it work the same? I can't find ABC."

". . . And finally she moved into one of those villages, you know, assisted living, down there in Milwaukee. Ellet, what's that place called that Leona's in down in Milwaukee . . . ?"

"Bingo. Look, he's still in the lead. This is my friend. We just played in an event on Wednesday, and we walked around with him the first three days. If he can hold on for three more holes, he's the champion."

"Friendship Village."

"That's it, Friendship Village. And who are you?"

"I'm from next door."

"We haven't met them yet."

"You'll like 'em. I'm the son-in-law."

"I saw another one who looked like a son-in-law."

"We all look alike. This isn't your favorite chair, is it?"

The Drakes turned out to be lovely hostage hosts. They didn't offer us anything to eat. That might have made us, if possible, more uncomfortable. In which case, we probably would have had to kill the Drakes. Make it look like a water-skiing accident.

Good news, bad news. Ellet and Fran Drake are on Sanibel Island now. And Peter Jacobsen put it in the pond in front of the eighteenth green. Fran was a little disappointed not to be able to tell people that a man who broke into her house knew the man who won the golf tournament in Chicago. And Fluff broke up with Peter. It wouldn't happen until years later, of course, but he decided to do it that day.

I felt completely responsible. If only family responsibilities hadn't taken me away. I would have shouted out, "Don't hit it in the water, Peter!" He'd have knocked it on, two putts; Fluff would have had 10 percent of a win and would never have known heartbreak with that fickle Tiger Woods character. It still haunts me.

It happened again. Years later I left Scott Simpson to win the L.A. Open by himself, which I thought would be good for him. This time it's a bartender at the hotel where my little sister's rehearsal dinner is being held.

"Hey, cool, you've got a big-screen TV . . . you watchin' the golf?"

"The golf?"

"Here's twenty dollars, please switch the station to NBC. Thank you."

"Okay."

And nobody has to die! I tune in just in time to see Scott walking up eighteen, needing a birdie to win. The camera walks along with him and he speaks into it, "Hey, Bill, I know you're out there. If I lose this thing, I'm holding you personally responsible. You're supposed to be here to relax me."

Well, he's loose enough, anyway. Let's hope he makes the birdie. But if the bartender is found later, the victim of a water-skiing accident, Scotty has given me the probable cause and motive.

Well Stadler wins 'cause Scott misses the putt, and again it's all my fault. I'm inconsolable, and not alone. The golf contingent of the family suggests perhaps we postpone the nuptials until after The Masters, but my sister and this guy she's going to marry say they want to go through with the ceremony anyway.

A big family fight breaks out. Everybody's shouting. I'm pleading with her to stand up to him. Pleading, "If he treats you like this on your wedding day, with all your brothers watching . . ." What can I say? She was a broken record—all about how it was *her* day; couldn't I think about *her* happiness? She looked lovely in her dress. They sent me pictures.

Gosh, I think I've built enough tension for the conclusion of my shoot-out in Chicago story. It's one of my favorites, and I sure hope you're ready now.

Mike Ditka was fun. He had a box of nice cigars to share. He had a little trouble keeping his emotions in check and after a bit the officials turned off his wireless microphone. Another way this format is tricky. Mike wasn't the only one new to an athletic event that was PG-13. When that sunk in, I think players began turning off their mikes as part of their pre-putt routine.

My mike stayed on and with it my running commentary, because I work clean, I don't do blue. The game within the format, or vice versa, was a modified Pinehurst where both teammates hit drives, then select one, and hit alternate shots from there. This moves things along; at the same time it encourages free swinging, which adds to the danger.

Critics complain that technical innovations have made the game too easy and that the modern game is bereft of danger. They're lying with numbers, folks; true, casualties are way down, but fatalities are through the roof. This day was throwback, this Pinehurst was old school.

One of the miracles of the game is you always end up on the green. I had hit no shots that I can remember, which is also a miracle; but I did can some putts. I made one sidehiller from the same point where Scott Simpson missed. I mention this not to brag, but only to remind him. It's been months.

One team was eliminated on each hole; in case of a tie, there'd be a chip-off or putt-off. These all made for fun. What with the microphone and all. Walking around that course that day, I saw how starved galleries are to be set free. It's not just the quiet, but also the golfers' tensions are mimicked. By physicalizing or simply acknowledging those tensions, you could effect crowd relaxation, warmth, and sometimes laughter.

It really was a lot of fun. At the penultimate hole, Peter made a nice putt, and suddenly all the teams had been eliminated except ours and the team of defending Western Open champion D. A. Weibring and Michael Jordan.

Until then, I'd been creeping along, trying not to be eliminated, very happy to still be playing. Kind of like dodgeball; you can make it to the end of the game not because you're so good but because no one has focused on you. Perhaps I wasn't perceived as a threat.

Well, if I was going down, I was going to dance with who brung me. I didn't talk in anyone's backswing, but it was close. And I made sure not to stand in an opponent's eyeline on the tee, by changing positions a few times. My courtesy was unsettling, as D.A. found an abandoned orchard of Mr. Butler's to the left and Michael discovered a creek to the right. The fairway wide open, Jacobsen in a cruel foreshadowing of Sunday found water at eighteen in what's now known as Michael Jordan Creek. With the competition and my partner thus in trouble, it only made sense to swing as hard as I've ever swung in my life.

Good idea. It started out straight, and it stayed straight for maybe seventy yards before it elevated, rising about a hundred and fifty feet in the air. Then it suddenly migrated, following Jordan Creek in search of Capistrano. It flew the creek, flew some very big trees, ending up beneath a branch, two, maybe three fairways over.

As we left the tee, my friend Bubba raced up to me with an opened *Sports Illustrated*. "You can do it, Billy. All you have to do is beat this guy here." The guy was Michael Jordan, photographed at work, grabbing a rebound, virtually his entire body at or above the rim. I swallowed and said, "You know that's the camera angle." Unfortunately, it felt like everyone in the gallery had seen the photograph. The crowd, the trees, and the glade gave me the momentary creeps that I was on my way out to duel with Aaron Burr, or some other unbeaten and untied bad boy.

They found D.A.'s ball in a good lie, and an urchin was showing off a fifty-dollar bill he'd found, saying, "Yeah, and he signed it, too." It's not just his offense or his defense, but M.J.'s indomitable will to win.

Mike chipped out, and Duck's Ass put it in the bunker right of the green. Jake hit his finest shot of the week, as far as I was concerned. From the shade, he walloped it

This is just a vanity shot.

. . . all of that one.

underneath that branch, between two trees, and tastefully into the fairway, throwing distance from the pin.

If only I could have thrown it. Or kicked it, or spit it, or something. Anything but hit it. In those days, I didn't have a lot of shots—caddy shots and the aforementioned throw, kick, and spit options.

I had one other. A flop shot I'd learned from Phil Rodgers at Grand Cypress. I did not have the presence of mind to stand in front of those six thousand people and act like I knew what I was doing. I just hit it, four feet away. Later tests showed blood in my urine, but no performance enhancers.

So that leaves Michael in the bunker. He wasn't the man he is today. He didn't have the turnaround jumper. He hadn't done all the upper-body work. His diet was different, he hadn't begun eating Cleveland Cavalier heart. He hadn't won the first of the six titles. He hadn't lost his father, he hadn't played with Rodman, he hadn't been photographed with that freak Bijan. All anybody knew was that he believed he could fly.

But would that be enough to beat me?

He stood there in that bunker for such a long time, just staring at the pin, that we all got scared. I told myself, "Relax, his nickname is Air, not Sand. Of course he'd been raised on the tidal mud flats of Wilmington. Perhaps he knew the secret language of the sand chiggers.

What if he'd convinced some hermit crab king to guide his shot into the cup? It was a very real possibility. The crowd's encouragement built to a roar till finally I asked, "Hey, just who are you people rooting for, anyway?"

They say that trial lawyers never ask a question that they don't already know the answer to. What am I, a lawyer?

It hurt so very fast, and so deep, kinda like "Are you going to go with me, or are you going with him?"

"I think maybe I'll go with him."

But also a bit like, "I guess the question is, do you still love me?"

"No, I guess I don't, come to think of it."

Don't let me forget, "Have you had anything to drink?"

"I had one beer, probably two hours ago."

"Would you mind stepping out of the car, sir?"

I couldn't even look at my mother. It had already been such a long struggle getting her to like me.

All these thoughts have gone through my head and Jordan's, still staring at the pin, looking like Lot's wife. I cave, I'm completely psyched, I'm just about to call out, "You can pick it up, that's good!"

When Mike swings, his ball flies about twenty yards in the air, almost lands in the cup on the fly, clanks off the pin, and bounces past. The crowd goes crazy, but Mike is not happy. And I am.

Aerobics with Phil Rodgers and the bodybuilding
Smothers.

"That's too bad, Mike. Especially since I got my pro hitting our next shot."

And what a pro. Peter knocked in the putt, a putt I would still be standing over today, and we were the champions. Out of nowhere. Cinderella story.

It was so unlikely, I could not stop laughing until they took me to the first-aid tent. We won a lot of money. For charity. But there is money that you earn, as salary, bonuses, investments, interest, theft; and then there's money that you win playing golf. Now that is real money.

I'm a sore loser, but incredibly gracious in victory. I must make a mention of my worthy adversary, Michael Jordan. He did his best. It had been a fun day, and people milled around for a long while. Autograph signing continued through a cigar and a drink or two afterward. Michael bore the brunt of it.

The city of Chicago was smitten with Mike, then to find out that he played golf too? This can make any relationship intensify from a crush to a fascination, to ardor, to infatuation, to worship. In Michael's case, it got a little weirder, as people ended up wanting to be like Mike.

No one was embarrassed to be wild for Mike, no matter how big he got. Nothing like Hanson backlash. Mike never had my problems. When I'm really down in a pit, I actually think, "Well, if I get the chance, I'll just jump in front of a bus to save a child, get pretty badly hurt, but refuse to talk about it. That will turn this whole thing around. Everybody will just get off my back."

"Hey, leave him alone. He's in the hospital, man."

"Yeah, maybe you'd feel a little differently about Bill if that had been your infant."

"For sure, it's not like he's asking for anyone's pity."

It's a lot of pressure, to be loved. You're expected to love back, and hell hath no fury like a fan scorned. Besides, there are aircraft carriers full of celebrities available for loving. Which provides the American public great freedom to be fickle. It's a cornerstone of this country. It's part of what makes us who we are.

If you were an Iraqi, your favorite celebrity would be: Saddam Hussein. Day in, day out, he's your guy. Because he's the only Iraqi celeb. He may invade, persecute, exterminate; his beret may reek of chemical weapons. He's still your guy. If Dick Van Patten moved to Iraq, you'd have an option. But I don't see that happening, do you?

If you're a Libyan, General Moammar Khadaffi is your man. You'll be getting his fan club newsletter no matter how crazy he dresses, or how often he changes his look. Libyan kids still have to tie their burnooses like him and give their hair bad dye jobs.

This is off the point, but Khadaffi is the only celebrity I can think of who looks as insane as people say he might be. Really. Sean Young? No. Orenthal James Simpson? Maybe up close. Stone Cold Steve Austin of the World Wrestling Federation? Heck no.

I went to Michael Jordan's first game in Madison Square Garden. In those days, the Bulls weren't a sellout, and neither was the Garden. My brother Brian and I bought tickets from scalpers who only took a little off the top and cleaned up around the ears.

Mike wasn't yet huge, but all the schoolyard knew him and they turned out in his haircut, too. In the Garden that night, there were probably four thousand guys with no hair. They either shaved it or didn't have it to begin with. And now they had a hero. Four thousand bulletheads. We stood outside after the game and just watched in awe. Perfectly natural. If I see four thousand of anything— geese, penguins, buffalo, mail trucks—I'm hypnotized. From humble beginnings, apparently this bullethead army went out, told others about Michael—and now him a big shot.

Michael Jordan has had a unique ability to remain likable, even selling Gatorade, batteries, and hamburgers. Check this out. He hawks Hanes underwear, comes off as a briefs man, but unaccountably doesn't disparage himself with men and women who prefer boxers. American voters switched to George Bush when they heard Bill Clinton wore boxers. When British heavyweight Frank

Bruno appeared at his weigh-in wearing lavender Euro-briefs, the Vegas odds for his fight with Mike Tyson were taken off the board.

Now Mike's talking on TV with Tweety Pie about how to save money on phone calls. Doing phone company ads is one of my graveyard destinations. Right before I do stand-up in Vegas. And *The Hollywood Squares*. How in the hell do these spokespersons know all about the phone rates? I hope somebody's keeping a seat warm in hell for them.

More likely, a *Bonfire of the Vanities* feel.

"Oh, look in the next car, the limo, it's, you know, from TV."

"Hi! Hello! We love you!"

"Stop and give us your autograph. We're huge fans."

"Here's an alley where we won't block traffic."

Then the horrible echo of boots kicking kidneys, hair and hair extensions being pulled from the skull, the harmonies of the voices of the disaffected, an excellent vintage of *The Grapes of Wrath*.

"Whatever happened to my one low monthly rate, sucker?"

"Here's a little something for your friends and family."

"Try this here for my weekend calls to Canada."

"Excuse me, my foot's just gotta reach out and touch you."

If you've been a Bulls fan since they were called the Chicago Zephyrs, it's nice to finally hold your head high. We don't admit that before the Zephyrs they were known as the Packers. The Chicago Packers. I suppose it could have been the Chicago Dolphins. It's a long way that Mike has taken us. A long distance.

Above and beyond the pleasure of watching him play. He gave all fans of basketball a rooting interest; and Chicagoans a rooting interest in the playoffs. He won those championships and brought back to Chicago the respect it hasn't had since Capone.

Michael Jordan is doing a movie, and he wants you to be in it. Heard it from my agent; the producer, our mutual friend. I had to hear it from Mike, though. He didn't know, he's not showfolk. You have to ask these things yourself. It was too much to ask to be asked by someone else. Will you do a film with Michael Jordan and the Tasmanian Devil?

Besides, many things are asked for in other people's names.

"Mom says it's okay if I take the car."

"Elvis wants to meet you in our van."

"The President wants you in a short skirt tonight."

"Jean-Claude Van Damme says that you are his favorite actor and that you should loan me two hundred dollars."

"Y'up?"

"Mmm, I'm up."

"Ya dressed?"

"Mmm, some."

"Some. That would be . . . ?"

"Socks and a T-shirt."

"Ya out of bed yet?"

"I'm getting up."

"Keep fightin', don't quit."

"I'm getting up right now. I'm up. I'm up."

"Take a standing eight count. Can you play?"

"Not completely sure. I don't hear anything down there."

"Well, that can be good . . . or real bad."

"That's what I thought."

"Find out and call me back."

"I'm afraid to go down there."

"You're the man of the house."

"That's why I'm afraid."

"You got to have a plan."

"Call back and I'll let it ring."

"And what do I say when they answer?"

"Hang up. But if nobody picks up, meet me in half an hour."

"Aren't you going to shower?"

"Can't take the chance. Shower there."

"This is a good plan."

"Hey, I *am* the man of this house."

The classic finish—navel pointed directly at the target.

I don't think I've ever had more fun on a golf course than when Bill and I beat D. A. Weibring and Michael Jordan in the shoot-out at the Western Open. The key moment was Bill's final shot. He hunkered in there, laid the blade back of his wedge, and then slipped into Carl Spackler mode: "The Cinderella Boy has come to Chicago," he said, "and he needs this shot to set up the victory." Then he took a big old Phil Mickelson swing, popped the ball up soft as you please, and dropped it straight down, four feet from the pin. It was a shot any pro would've been proud of. Bill then ran into the bunker, fell to his knees, and pumped his fist several times. At the prize ceremony, slack-lipped Carl returned. "For years, the Chicago sports establishment has tried to hold me back—Wrigley, Reinsdorf, Halas—they've all tried to stop me—but they can't stop me now. I'm one of the greatest athletes in Chicago history, and it's my turn now. I'm going all the way." Bill did go all the way for the fans that day, and I don't think anyone who was there will ever forget it.

—*Peter Jacobsen*

And if someone else asks a favor for you, you don't have to owe that person back. That's Accounting 101.

When Mike himself asked, I said yes. But he doesn't owe me. Much. Daffy Duck was such a pain in the ass. You see, I already owed him from that day of golf at Butler.

It was late, dark, everybody was filing out, and I saw Michael, quietly slipping out of the clubhouse via the pro shop. "Say, Michael," I implored. And I saw the body language in his back. He'd been caught. He was tired, and tired of signing autographs. He just wanted to get in his car and play the music loud and go home to his wife and kids. He turned around, and I asked him anyway.

"Would you please take a picture with my mother and sister?"

And that bastard said, "No way, fool." Got in his Porsche and drove away.

Golly, wouldn't that be a sad story: "Then I took a six-iron to his anterior cruciate ligaments—went to prison for it. He ended up in a wheelchair for life, the Bulls never won a title, and Nike stayed as big as Keds."

No, Mike came back. Put his big arms around my girls and turned on those runway lights he's got for a smile. They all lit up. They knew it looked funny and that it would never happen again. That's why I asked.

Laura, my brother Michael, and our mom.

Thursday

This morning, at the same time that I put on my socks, shoes, and ear muffs, I slip on my game face. The bell has rung; it's time to tee it up for real. Side by side with the play-for-pay boys.

I can handle it. I'm used to these guys. My pro days go back to 1964 when some of us caddies pulled duty as standard-bearers at the Western Open. Standards are signs on poles displaying the players' current scores. You march around with the standard and stay out of everybody's way.

My friend Bob Schriver was a shrubbery cardplayer, sometime smoker, and St. Francis Xavier wise-ass. He knew Mike Dann, a Loyola guy one year ahead of me whose dad was the Executive Director of the Western Golf Association, which put on the tournament. Bob played good golf, too, one year making it to the U.S.

Amateur. But as a suck-up, Schriver was a scratch. Some kids imprint their fathers; others, sports heroes. Bob encoded Mr. Eddie Haskell. I believe it was two days after another buddy of mine, Bucky Benz, and I saw him walking around with—and dressed identically to—Mike Dann that Bob weaseled the pole position in the Arnold Palmer threesome.

Arnold is and was the king. Incandescent, perhaps the dominant personality in the history of the game. He had style, he played boldly, he was never out of it. He and Patton were born to lead armies. Arnie could bring a gallery close to him, involve them, make them think with him and feel his pain. And when it worked, they'd get the payoff—the Palmer grin. Those Latrobe choppers worked magic. It's no wonder Arnie still plays golf with his dentist.

And there Palmer was, on the next fairway, where Bob Schriver was helping him with club selection. He'd nod his head as Arnie pulled a club from the bag. The fraud even moved his lips, "That's the club, A.P. Trust it." He couldn't look over at me. No, they were too focused on winning the tournament.

The guys on the boards I toted were not only in black numbers but double-digit black. Bucky's were, too. During the tournament, we'd wave our doleful numbers at each other, sharing the shame. But something did happen in the practice rounds. We tagged along with Jack

Nicklaus, pacing off yardages for him that he'd record in his course Bible. He didn't smile much and had no army, but he was all ours. And he had game.

There he was, hemmed in by our motley group, and someone called out, "Who are you guys?" Bucky snapped back, "We're Jack's Pack!" Nicklaus turned, surprised, and smiled. Major Columbus, Ohio, porcelain. All he'd needed was a collective noun.

That week Bucky screamed, "Jack's Pack!" after every good shot. The gallery picked it up, and by the end of the week there were signs. Bucky Benz later had his name legally changed, by an orthodontist, to Johnny; but no matter—he'd coined "Jack's Pack."

The climax of this tournament changed the way I'd look at golf. Palmer was the favorite, and he was at or around the lead the whole week. But a little-known player stayed with him, making birdies, and finally the distant shouts were too much to ignore. I came upon his excited gallery just as he was putting. I couldn't see, could only hear the roar as his ball neared and dropped into the cup. Then the crowd heaved and I poked my head through. A guy in a white Panama hat raised his putter high above his head, then whirled it like a sword before sheathing it in an imaginary scabbard at his side. He held it there and marched like a matador while the crowd went silly with joy. "My gosh," I thought, "this guy is not like the other guys, is he?"

Several years ago at Pebble Beach, I got into a conversation with Bill, and the subject drifted onto charities. I mentioned that I was involved with a Children's Hospital in my hometown of St. Louis and said something like "Bill, if you're ever so inclined, we'd love to have your support." That evening, when Sally and I returned to our room, we found at our door one of the commemorative liquor decanters that all AT&T contestants receive, empty, with a note inserted in the top. It said: SORRY, I JUST COULDN'T HELP MYSELF—BILL. Attached to the note was a very generous check made out to HALE'S HOSPITAL. A couple of years later, Bill came out to the fund-raiser we hold each summer and not only played in the event but dominated the charity auction that night, acting as part emcee/part bidder. He ended up outbidding himself for the last item of the night—a framed collection of signed golf gloves from the Presidents Cup team I captained in 1994. Then he gave it back to me. "I want you to hang it in the hospital," he said. "But if you ever redecorate, I want it back."

—*Hale Irwin*

Kids are the coolest: the ones on the top are my favorites.

Chi Chi Rodriguez dueled Arnold Palmer till the final hole of the final round. He had hung with the king and then held him off, delighting a rollicking Chicago golf crowd. I'll never forget the eighteenth green at Tam O'Shanter. Rodriguez had a birdie putt to clinch. He stepped up, looked at it for one second, and rapped it with his Bull's-eye. It fell in, Chi Chi raced to the cup and covered it with his Panama. As the crowd screamed, he tentatively peeked under the hat to see if the ball was still there. Relieved, he spread his arms wide and gutted the sky from lips to hips.

He had more fun playing golf than any person I'd ever seen. And he'd given more fun. He had won the tournament, holding off the great Palmer while putting on a show of golf joy. He did most of it without words, like a dancer or clown.

Golf entertainment (I've said it, pay no attention) is part landscape painting—the defined space, the natural amphitheater of each green and tee. The eye is invited to see golfer as celebrant. It is satisfying, and a sense of order, harmony, and security is conveyed.

What good fortune that the Senior Tour came along for Chi Chi Rodriguez. And vice versa. He thrived, it thrived. These days, as his game mellows, the putts at eighteen aren't for the title; they're for the early birds claiming prime bleacher spots.

I saw Chi Chi a few years ago in the grill room of my home club, Sleepy Hollow. He had a beer, and a faraway look. Like an old comic at the Friar's Club. Perhaps people had stopped asking about the things he wished to talk about. Signing autographs on golf balls, that wasn't his metier. He did landscapes. Big ones.

The AT&T Pebble Beach National Pro-Am has a lot going for it—surreal surroundings, exhilarating courses, fresh shellfish. Good God, it's *National.*

A few years back, I got invited to play in the Greater Milwaukee Open Pro-Am. The letter was quite amusing. "We're a small tournament, we have no TV, we've lost some sponsors, and we've also lost our site; we'll be playing this year on a public course. If there's any way you could make it, we sure would appreciate it."

This arrow somehow got through my chain mail. I phoned Milwaukee and a guileless woman verified the whole sob story. The event was months away, so forty minutes passed discussing badger beer, bars, brats, bands, and state troopers.

"August is beyond the range of my crystal ball," I said, "but it's possible. If I can make it, I will. It's been very nice talking to you. What's your name, ma'am?"

"Marion. What's yours?"

"I like the name Marion. My name is Bill Murray."

"Are you *the* Bill Murray?"

"Well, I'm *a* Bill Murray."

"Okay. Hope you can make it. Bye-bye."

"Bye-bye."

Two months later, I'm in Woodruff, Wisconsin, and quite disappointed. We'd gone for breakfast to Paul Bunyan's. There was a queue, and the sign said ALL YOU CAN EAT. My two big boys and I had left St. Paul after an evening baseball game, driven all night, and arrived hungry. When finally seated at the pine plank tables, we were served coffee in camp cookware—metal cups with a speckled blue enamel finish. And set on the table was a bowl of doughnuts. We Murrays must have cops in our background 'cause those doughnuts disappeared quickly. Coffee was refilled and a flashing busgirl piped "More doughnuts?"

"Well, if they're already made . . ."

Columbo or Quincy would have noticed. "More doughnuts?" How many times have you heard that in a restaurant? And we heard it again before we ordered. They were fabulous, fresh doughnuts, and we'd each had seven before our breakfast arrived. Any American eating in Paul Bunyan's feels a mighty obligation to fortify himself, lest the Great Lakes suddenly need redigging. Three dozen eggs, six rashers of bacon, a side of ham, a haystack of pancakes, and a whole watermelon. I wasn't crazy about the breakfast, and didn't finish it, either. As we left, chastened, we realized that all those people in line out front had come solely to buy the doughnuts.

From the pay phone in Pauly's parking lot, an officious man's voice: "Greater Milwaukee Open."

"Yes, I'd like to know what time the Pro-Am starts tomorrow morning, and if there's practice range to hit on early."

"That information should be in the packet that was sent to you, sir."

"No packet was received. See, I wasn't sure I'd be able to come . . ."

"If you did not receive a packet . . . you are not playing in the Pro-Am, sir. The packets were sent out a month ago, and everyone who is playing has received theirs."

"But I was invited, and I called a couple of months ago . . ."

"A . . . couple . . . of . . . months . . . ago . . ."

"And I think I received letters after that . . ."

"You talked to someone a couple of months ago, sir? The packets were sent out to all those playing in the Pro-Am. If you did not receive a packet . . ."

"But I think they're expecting me."

"You are not expected, sir. No one is expecting you. I guarantee you. If you did not receive a packet, then you are not expected."

". . . Is there a Marion there?"

"Hold on, please."

About a minute passed in Bunyan's gravel lot. Then a sweet woman's voice came across the phone.

"Is this *a* Bill Murray?"

It was a nice bunch of guys to play with. Jim Gallagher, Jr., was the pro, along with three Milwaukee studs: Ed Bechtold, John Bowlin, and Terry "The Judge" Evans. There were Packer fans everywhere, and in my Jehovah's Witness way, I think I touched them. "Have you heard about the Chicago Bears? Would you like to receive some literature?"

We finished the round, and that's all. Quietly, very quietly, the grandstands at eighteen stared at us as we putted out. John Bowlin was the general at the Planck Road Brewery, and his MPs took us directly to the bar. State law says all brewery employees must drink a wooden leg's weight in beer at all public social functions. I hunkered. Ours is a nation of laws.

One extremely good citizen said I had to make it over to the rib tent, that the ribs were the best I'd ever taste. He later slobbered that if I didn't make it to the rib tent, it would be a wasted trip, and why had I bothered coming, anyway. But he didn't want that to happen and he was going to see to it that I went home with some ribs.

In Milwaukee, dress native.

Grace and beauty at the old Number 5.

I still can't quite believe what I saw at the tenth tee of Poppy Hills a few years back. The gallery was two or three deep and Bill as usual was doing his best to keep everyone entertained. He had a tee in his hand, and at one point he flicked it playfully in the direction of Mark Grace, who was on the other side of the tee box, maybe twenty-five feet away. The tee sailed through the air, end over end, straight at Grace's face, but he saw it coming, and he caught it. But not in his hand—he caught it between his teeth! It was the most incredible thing I've ever seen. I think Bill then deadpanned something like "Ladies and gentlemen, *please* don't try this at home."

—*R. J. Harper,*
Director of Golf,
The Pebble Beach Company

My civic duty fulfilled, I headed to the parking lot where brother Johnny Murray, designated driver, slept in the RV before blastoff to New York. Suddenly there was Socrates again, to escort me to the rib tent. Inside were a hundred people with a six-hour headstart on me. Maybe seven. I grabbed a rib, surprised to find it even better than advertised. And got the hell out of there. I've been to Milwaukee before. I know what can happen.

Oh, I almost forgot. My caddy, Jerry Huffman, was a smiling, happy guy. When I asked him if he had any more of that stuff back at the caddyshack, he said, "I'm not a caddy, I work at the NBC affiliate. I'm the one who wrote, inviting you." After my escape from rib Sodom, he handed me something wrapped in a long tube sock. "Just as I promised in my last letter," he said. It was a Louisville Slugger. I didn't understand, as I hadn't read the last letter, or the one before that. They'd gone into the "answer when answerable" stack. "I said that if you came to Milwaukee I'd get you one of these." The autograph beneath the emblazoned name made me gasp. Henry Aaron. The man Ernie Banks said was the best player he ever saw. The Hammer. Number 44.

My head cracked and the light came in. I saw, clearly, my first trip to Milwaukee.

*　*　*

Late September, 1957. "Get in the car, we're going for a ride." Magic words to kids in a crowded house. All nine kids—no wait, 1957, how many were there, six, seven? We didn't ask where we were going, but after a while we noticed that Dad was listening to the ball game and it wasn't the Cubs but the Braves. We crossed the state line and kept driving on to downtown Milwaukee. When the game ended, the Braves had won the National League pennant and a party broke out. Streets jammed with honking cars. *Happy Days* couples stood in open convertibles and screamed the names of the Braves. Eddie Mathews! Warren Spahn! Henry Aaron!

The bat wasn't expected, and wasn't needed, but I accepted it. You see, it wasn't remuneration, or tribute, but remembrance. The bat's always with me now. And if you bump my recreational vehicle in traffic, or cut me off or flip me off, I'll just reach under the seat and wave it to you. A couple folks towing U-Hauls got to see it on the way back to New York.

I didn't play for about a month, and my clubs were still in the RV. One Saturday I tossed them into the car, and when I arrived at the course I said to the caddy, "Check the bag, will you? I think there's a wet towel or something in there."

At Sleepy Hollow, the first tee is overlooked by the terrace outside the grills, the pro shop, and the caddy depar-

My childhood summers were all about baseball. I played nearly every day. We'd ride an hour from home on bikes to find a ballpark with home run fences. I'd spend hours at night making phone calls to round up eighteen players. That was the ultimate—two full teams for a pickup game. It would blow kids' minds; they'd show up and see all these good players. You look up and there's five more guys on bikes who've come from the other side of town. Hit to all fields, first base out, no pitcher's hands. It gave me a great sense of accomplishment. As adults we move away from games with eighteen players.

ture lounge. Weekends, fifty or sixty onlookers watch you tee off. My foursome was already on the tee, and the looper was rooting around in the bag when I came down the steps to grab some tees and a scorecard.

To my left, I heard a guttural grunt, then the sound of something dropping. From above me on the parapet, a swarm began buzzing. I looked up to see a frozen group stare. It didn't feel good. I looked over to see another tableau, with one moving part. My caddy is flipping Saran Wrapped handfuls of ribs out onto the tee and he's frightened, because the ribs are also gift-wrapped in a green vapor billowing from the side zipper pocket.

Put yourself in my shoes. Everybody comfy? You know, this is where club membership becomes so important. As a guest, I'd have been forced to disavow ownership of the bag until down the fairway and out of sight of the clubhouse. This would save my member sponsor from shame. But as a proud member, I was able to march to my caddy and crisply announce, "The sun's coming out. We won't be needing those today."

Friday

I've just had a Monterey red wine remembrance: Smothers, like the brothers. My first run-in with the Brothers Smothers was at the Grand Cypress Resort in Orlando. After a few years, I'd become frustrated with cooler golf. That is, load cooler on golf cart, play golf while emptying the cooler. Me and the cooler would be fine till about the thirteenth hole when the wayward shots began to come in rapid succession. Sufficiently coolered, I would be unable to reverse this trend, and a storm cloud of hubris and juice-induced wagers would drown me till round's end.

I saw an ad in a golf rag for the golf school at Grand Cypress. The school was run then as now by Fred Griffin, a great American from the state of Georgia. I showed up for school bright and early one Monday morning. Well, actually, last but not least.

I think there were eight of us in the class, and as I jumped from my moving golf cart, I saw the confusion and regret on the faces of a couple of my schoolmates. As I shook hands down the line, I speed-bumped on the explanation—Dick and Tom Smothers.

When you think golf with union guys, you think Frank Fitzsimmons of the Teamsters Union, not the members of SAG, AFTRA, and AGVA. It may be interesting but probably very bad luck. I once settled into the first-class section of a flight to see Tony Curtis, Ann-Margret, and Henny Youngman seated around me. "Oh my God," I thought, "it's *Airport '75*. We're all going down!"

Fortunately, everybody at Grand Cypress got their tuition's worth in golf and entertainment. There were tidal waves of laughter in those few days, topping my previous high—junior year Spanish class with Señor Alan Berkson.

Señor Alan was a first-time high school teacher from whom I'd taken first-year Spanish in summer school. I'd excelled in that class, and when I drew him again for junior year, I expected great grades and maybe learning, God forbid. I was glad that I arrived early for that first class. One at a time, students entered. Each one would have qualified for the Cuban Boatlift (and another of my favorite classes, American-Castro history).

Me and Hooter with his vehicle.

Fidel had announced that Cubans wishing to could emigrate to America. Every guy on the Eastern seaboard with a boat drove down to Key West, where Cuban-Americans with fistfuls of cash were booking passages for relatives in Cuba. Charter skippers, arriving in Cuba for their manifest, were forced to take three passengers for every one they had contracted for. Free of charge. Well, that sounds merciful enough, except Fidel Castro selected the passengers he wished to send to Jimmy Carter's America. We are a big bully country, with a knack for getting our way. Amen. But sometimes we Yankees are snookered by a roaring mouse.

It's a Key West tradition to view the sunset from Land's End, southernmost point of the continental forty-eight. A mixed crowd of stoners and naturalists *ooh* and *aah* at the very fine semi-tropical light show. Crowds were unusually heavy the week of the Boatlift with anxious relatives and curious locals hoping to meet the new arrivals. Heavy seas offshore had reportedly swamped several unseaworthy craft, and the "Freedom Flotilla" was limping in, Dunkirk style.

As the boats chugged by the breakfront, the onlookers froze in midwave at the sight of Castro's largesse. The deportees fell into three categories: the physically handicapped, career criminals, and the mentally insane. Picture it. Dangerously overloaded boats teeming with the wretched refuse of an enemy state, spectacularly backlit by the beacon of our solar system. The joke going around town was, "Hey, did you check out today's sunset?"

Now you can't compare these kinds of terrifying immigrants with my first-year Spanish class. No. In order to do that, you would have to know all the people aboard the boats. But it was something like the first get-together of the Dirty Dozen, or the gleeful realization of the party possibilities aboard Con Air.

Arklike, missing only the female partners, came every miscreant student type in the school. Tee-hee laughter led to groans of pity for the as-yet-unsized-up teacher. Roars of glee at the comic possibilities with each new addition. The cunning, the sly, the lazy, the insipid, the downright dense, the sinister, the cruel, the dangerous, the underachieving, the sons of benefactors, starting football players, the notably flatulent, the unkempt, the gross, the drunk, the weary, the angry, and the already suicidal.

The screams brought teachers from down the hall, each ready to mete out Jesuit justice. But none had the guts. They turned and left as if going to get backup; but none came. What they saw sickened and frightened them.

I've seen the look just one other time, while boating with Hunter Thompson. We arrived at his boat, which hadn't

I was so relieved—literally—when Bill arrived on the AT&T Pebble Beach scene. For years I'd served as the tournament's comic relief, and I was wearing out my yo-yos. Now Bill is the show, and what a show he is! One year my group played just in back of his—and for three days I got heckled by gallery members delivering lines Bill had fed them. And unlike just about everyone else in the tournament, the more Bill communes with the gallery, the better he seems to play. I'll never forget the year he made the cut for the first time. My wife and I had gone to dinner that night at Club XIX, one of the restaurants in The Lodge. Out on the patio, a jubilant Bill was holding court at a long table that included Scott Simpson, Jeff Sluman, and assorted Murray relatives and friends. Much Merlot had been consumed, and much more was to follow. I sat down with them just long enough for the group to pick me up—chair and all—for a brief celebratory ride. They were all still there after we'd finished dinner. The next morning I think Bill had some problems focusing on his putts, but he and Scott still finished among the leading teams, and I wasn't surprised. My old golf school-mate had a terrific swing even before the Grand Cypress guys got to him, and he's even better now. In fact, with his talent, the only way he can justify that sixteen handicap is if he putts every day like a man with a hangover.

—*Tommy Smothers*

Kevin Scott, Nancy Brumbaugh, Wayne Yamagiwa, and a couple of other marshals took their badges off to join Scott and me for a sandbaggers' necktie party.

been used in a few days. It was hot, and our beer needed quick stashing. The starboard cooler, sadly, was found to contain last week's chum, which the tropics had turned into maggots. The sight—well, okay—the sight. But the smell, the smell was the smell of many, many million deaths. Instinctive horror, and it was chucked into the water.

But we were in a harbor, docked at rest; and the scum of the chum and the maggot spawn flotsam landed and simply stared right back. Like bridesmaids' vomit at a stoplight. It seemed like hours but was probably only twelve seconds before the living school of stench began to move, settling two slips down.

Poor bastard smelled it before he saw it. Roars of outrage and fright and disgust. When the slap of small waves began splashing funky, squirming larvae up to the gunwales of his pleasure craft, we felt a cold beer outside the reef would help. The abrupt takeoff of the twin 195s made any formal introductions to a day's generations of maggots impossible. We certainly couldn't have remembered every name.

So yes, I'm the kind of person you can meet when you attend a golf school. Made some mistakes, sure. We broke that Señor Berkson, but some class would have; and I bet that guy we left our maggots with dined out on that story for years. The debts have all been paid. Let's tee it up sometime. Let's definitely do that.

Anyway, it was a lot of fun with Dick and Tom. And Phil Rodgers, short game master and guest instructor at the school. That week Phil knew his grapes. The brothers, who are sibling vintners way funnier than Ernest & Julio Gallo, would open bottles, and Phil and I would finish them. "Rodney Strong is strong. Old Rodney, he's strong," Phil would say.

And then it would be morning, a little later each morning. The final day my arrival was by hotel van ambivac, its sliding door opened to ram-air needed oxygen to my crippled brain and organs. There, in a bunker teaching kindergartners, stood Rodgers. Ninety degrees, breathing under his own power with sweat that tasted mature, vibrant, oaky, and fruity. That is the difference between an amateur and a professional.

Nowadays at Grand Cypress, there's less schooling, more fooling. "We're having so much fun. Why fritter away time trying to learn golf?" Fred has passed this on to his many fine young teaching pros, who require sorely needed life lessons. The facets of a dozen PGA solitaires have been polished with my worldliness, and Griffin's country wisdom.

Fred hails from the Georgia country profiled by Charles Kuralt in his *On the Road* series. Denizens there eat a local jambalaya of red clay, ants, and dirt. It hasn't hurt him any. He's loved and respected, and has his Popsicles all to himself. Got a lovely wife, too, and children who eat hamburgers and hot dogs.

We usually end up in a restaurant called Hemingway's. There, we demand "a big ole, big ole piece'a groupah. Biggest slab'a groupah you kin cut." To walk in and see a whole grouper in the refrigerated glass case with a note just above his fish eye—I AM RESERVED FOR BILL MUR-RAY—well, it's a good feeling, one that carries over to the next day's golf.

The National at Augusta is a pretty nice golf course, too, for a cathedral. There is no real rough there—just "second cut" once a year. They wouldn't know what to do with long grass. Insects live in rough, and it can be so unkempt-looking. If a cone falls from a Georgia pine, an alarm goes off at the greenkeeper's manse, and a truck is dispatched to the offending area.

On my first visit to The Masters, I was warned not to bring any attention to myself, and I dressed down accordingly. With an oversized tennis hat pulled over my eyes and a pair of post-cataract-removal sunglasses, I felt confident I was looking my least. We walked out to seventeen, where the Golden Bear was arriving at the green. He made par, and with his son Jackie as caddy, marched over to the eighteenth tee. There was a wait to tee off, and Jack stood looking at the gallery.

Before I got good at golf.

Kevin McKinney, Fred "Groupah" Griffin, Eric Eshleman, and I in *Rushmore II*.

People used to being surrounded develop an extrasensory ability to recognize an outsider or a weirdo. When I'm working on a movie set, I can feel the presence of someone who doesn't belong. They've just got a different, nonworking, absorbent vibe.

Jack conferred with Jackie and then gestured in my direction. My hair stood on end as the gallery followed the Bear's glare. Since he wasn't smiling, the concern was that Jack's legendary focus had been distracted. This was not good for golf, or America. Heads whipped back and forth from Jack to the general area in which he was looking. "Is someone bothering Jack?"

He spoke, almost loud enough to hear, and gestured again in my direction. This made the gallery honk like geese. "Somebody is bothering Jack! Somebody is bothering Jack!" A couple of vigilantes started sidling my way, standing next to random suspects, "Is this the guy?" My mouth got dry and I thought I might retch the bad ham biscuit I'd had for breakfast.

Just before they got to me, Jack spoke again, this time his gaze fixed so certainly upon me that the crowd around backed off, expecting gunplay.

"I think it's about a six-iron," he said.

I was confused, we all were confused, because it didn't sound like "Bring me the head of that gentleman in the hat and bad glasses." He gestured again, indicating the

Please, for God's sake, get up.

We're playing in the 1998 JAL Big Apple Classic Pro-Am, and our "D" player, Ty Votaw, now the Commissioner of the LPGA, is facing a tough wedge shot from a downhill lie. So Bill steps directly behind him and starts coaching him on alignment. "Okay, turn a bit to the right . . . more right . . . more right." Eventually the poor guy is aiming down the first-base line for a shot that needs to go to left-center field. He has no chance, and no one knows that better than Bill who keeps saying, "More right . . . more right." Finally, with Votaw contorted like a pretzel and all but unable to take the club back, Bill delivers his coup de grace: "Are you ready to accept Jesus Christ as your personal savior?"

—*Bob Schwartz,*
Vice President/Marketing,
Golf Magazine Properties

distance from the tee to the eighteenth green, about 400 yards uphill.

"I think it's about a six-iron."

Jack, the last place I would have expected it—on the eighteenth at Augusta—had made a funny. I was as surprised as I could be surprised. I gave all signs of appreciation of his gesture, at the same time assuming jungle-kingdom subservient postures to indicate that I was no threat to Jack, golf, or the Republic. He smashed his drive down the fairway, smiled, and led his migration toward distant watering holes.

I played the National, too. I'd forgotten to bring a putter and was kindly allowed to field-test one of the pro shop's. There was a reason the putter hadn't been sold. Although I was hitting the ball well, my score was tumorous. I would finish with sixty-three putts. I hit some from on the green past the pin and off the green. I hit some from off the green past the pin and off the green. I hit some from off the green to the pin and back down off the green, farther away than when I'd started. I hit them from on the green, past the pin and into the water. Finally, at the famous fifteenth, a par-five over water, I reached the green in two with a monstrous drive and four-iron. I was putting for eagle at fifteen, where Masters are won and lost, where the green jackets get tailored.

Let's see, one in the ocean, two out, three in the trap, four in the grandstand, five back in the ocean. Think I'll let Scotty handle this one.

I missed the eagle putt. I missed the birdie putt. I missed the par putt. I held it in for about thirty yards. Then I hurled that worthless Bull's-eye straight up into the air over my head as Japanese golfers do when they commit hara-kiri. Of course, with this crummy putter, the blade did not mercifully slip into my skull, but instead stuck thirty feet up in the wisteria that wraps around the beautiful tree shading the sixteenth tee.

For about twenty seconds, it stayed there before dropping ten feet closer to the ground. Another ten seconds and it dropped ten more feet. Then twice more in this heart-sickening fashion until it was home in my hands, safe, sound, never to leave again. Although on sixteen, when I putted the ball into the pond, I thought about buying the putter so I could leave it with my golf ball.

Saturday

It's dawn at the big course, Pebble, and the only guys out are on mowers. As the thin John Deere hum reaches my balcony, my thoughts drift back to my own days behind the wheel of one of mankind's most treasured pieces of machinery.

After my father died, a decent fellow parishioner named William Klinge set me up with a job at the Evanston Community Golf Course. ECGC, as no one called it, crisscrossed the drainage canals whose source was Lake Michigan and final destination was the Gulf via the Chicago, the Illinois, and the Mississippi. So we felt a part of something bigger.

They were unglamorous drainage canals then; today they're protected wetlands, important migratory stop-overs for mice and frogs. In those days, however, we greenkeepers were the only protectors. We left the animals to take care of themselves; we had to protect the golf course. Not just from your standard high school vandal, but from the golfers.

I don't know if security guards should have guns, or public school teachers, either. But I can make a case that golf course rangers be issued shotguns with popcorn-packed shells. Not for killing, but maiming, maybe. A midsummer week in Bermuda shorts with a nasty kernel rash on the back of the legs will do wonders for a moron.

There must be a bent chromosome somewhere in man that urges him to wound that which he can't conquer, deface that which is more beautiful, misunderstand and befoul the work of another. The maintenance laws of golf—replace your divot, repair ballmarks on greens— are not just courtesies to the golfers who will follow nor simple respect for those who made the course what it is. They function as antidote to the suffering that golf provides a man in the moment that he sees how good a golfer he is at the same time that he sees how good a golfer he thinks he is.

Please let me examine one of my habits. I overdo the dictum: "On every green, repair your ballmark and one other." Instead of lining up my putt, I'm giving the bent grass a facial. Why? Help me.

It's not objective duty, as someone once said about refilling an emptied ice cube tray; but it does feel good,

Showing the folks at Spyglass how to pick up the 7–10 split.

One word: Nuts!

Bill will go the distance, however far, to achieve the ultimate comedic moment. In the eight years I've caddied for him at the AT&T, I've seen this countless times, but never more vividly than on the Saturday at Pebble Beach when he decided he needed a beer. I told him the thirteenth green would be a good spot, as I had friends there who would be delighted to accommodate. As we approached the green, a rowdy crowd of five hundred or so began cheering for Bill. It happened to be the Santa Clara University branch of his fan club. They were all wearing T-shirts emblazoned SAVE THE SANTA CLARA FOOTHILLS and they had one for Bill, which he immediately donned. Then he played with them a bit, made a few jokes, and generally entertained before putting out. Meanwhile, his beer had been procured. As he arrived at the back of the green, I handed it to him and asked him to acknowledge my friends. Ever gracious, he looked their way and raised his cup in thanks as they raised theirs in return. But these formalities only reignited the fans. As Bill brought the cup to his lips, they chanted, "Go! Go! Go!" Standing behind him, I whispered, "You know, you have to finish that," but as usual he was way ahead of me. While grimacing, he downed the beer like a collegiate brew-guzzling champion, then spiked the cup into the green before exiting stage rear as the crowd cheered its triumphant hero.

—*Andrew Whitacre,*
Bill's Caddy at the
AT&T Pebble Beach National Pro-Am

like taking out the trash, or loading the dishwasher. This good feeling, I imagine, will lead me to peace, making me ready to putt. At the same time, restoring the grass places me in harmony with the leprechaun who lives within the green, and he might give me a break on a sidehill slider.

I mean it's possible, right? They say it's not the read, it's the confidence in the stroke. If one's cool with the landscape, or even just the landscapers . . . but this may not be the mental game everybody else is playing, and I need to know. I need feedback.

Moving on. The head greenkeeper, Bob Ruley, was a fireman. Most of the workers were firemen. Evanston firemen worked one full day, then had two days off. Those days they worked on the golf course. Their firehouse was next to the starter's shack and the first tee. The entire course was dotted and surrounded by landmarks, which gave the job site the feeling of a gameboard.

The course straddled the village line between Evanston and Wilmette, with the Great Lake just beneath the horizon to the east. The north end of the course bordered Wilmette's Gilson Park, where I first played Little League, went to the beach, and parked in cars with girls who drank Seagram's 7. We were also the first to steal the Gilson Park sign.

That theft required membership in an idle brain society, fuel for courage, of course. Humorous men and attractive women dressed as dacoits; and a well-laid plan ending with a party worthy of all that danger and daring. There is something very sexy about a decent guy who just got mixed up in the heist of a city park sign.

As my mind looks across Sheridan Road, I can see the pasty-faced nightcrawler I was, dim now in the colossal shadow thrown by the bronzed forearm, sweaty and grass-clipping-spattered, wage-earning boy toy of three decades ago.

On this par-62 layout would be fought a great battle for respectability. By no means the decisive battle—years of trench warfare would ensue—and the symbol of that victory's reward rose just east, at the foot of Linden Street.

The Bahai Temple, Wilmette, Illinois, has a companion temple on the exact opposite point of the globe in India. The Bahai faith started in the nineteenth century, near Persia, I think. I'll check. The prophet was named Baha-ullah. The faith believes in the unity of all religions, the nine major ones celebrated in the nine sides of the temple. Bahais are victims of genocide in Persia. Where's that logic? Choose no favorites; believe all faiths are equal in God's eyes? Okay, prepare to die for that belief.

The Bahais I've met were all the coolest, most accepting people. The only famous Bahais are Seals and Croft. Their biggest hit, "Summer Breeze," received so much airplay for so many years that I became sick of it.

Don't put this on the Internet. There are weirdos out there.

I'm embarrassed by the words I have just written. I will make amends. From this day forth, I will not react negatively upon hearing the opening strains of "Summer Breeze." Instead, I will quiet myself and, quite sure I know the words, sing along. My conscious suffering of this song will turn it into a prayer offered in the name of ending the religious persecution of these gentle people. There, it's not even 11 A.M., and I've got my good deed for the day out of the way.

But now I hear a voice questioning my sincerity. And not yours, either, gentle reader, but one of my own. I know this voice. This voice occasionally reminds me of the year I gave up rock candy for Lent. Rock candy. Still couldn't do it. I am not enjoying the implicit tone of this voice, so I've gotten up and changed the station to the '70s hits. Which is also a religion, but not major. And now I can be in the occasion of singing.

The temple. This powerful majesty towers over the golf course, giving hint at meaning. It is Wilmette's most famous beauty, if you disqualify Ann-Margret Olsson for hyphenating. It suggests a world view beyond this village; that achievement and understanding just may need to be searched for elsewhere.

Of course, I'm just working on a golf course. On any gameboard, you need the right game piece to play. That was decided over breakfast at Mr. Eddie's. Mr. Eddie was not from this country or this continent. That's all I knew; we never sat down and talked. Our crew had bacon or sausage with eggs and hash browns, every single day. One guy would pick up all the checks. Usually Ruley, least often the junior member.

Toothpicks in mouth, we'd walk under the El tracks past the National Guard quonset to our vehicle sheds. Ruley allowed only the firemen to cut the fairways, so they drew the Ford tractors that pulled the gang mowers. Ruley used his car, or a backhoe or tractor, or stayed on foot. That left the red Jeep truck and a blue roofless '50s Willys Jeep.

Downshifting the Willys to jump a curb after an arm-signaled left turn—cutting the engine and jumping out at a slow roll—pretty much said everything I had to say. There was one car in the neighborhood with a competitive vocabulary. It was parked in the interns' lot of Evanston Hospital, kitty-corner from Mr. Eddie's. It was a red, maybe '67 Triumph convertible with a black peace symbol aft of the front wheel well. It was the only car in those parts with one. That car spoke to me. A good car, and a good idea, and they went together. I found a sub-text, too: You can have a job of service and be well paid for it. There's no reason they can't go together.

There was an old guy who beat the bushes for golf balls. He was not a golfer, and it bothered me that he entered on foot and reclaimed balls our golfers could have found. My first week on the job I pulled up next to him in the Jeep. "Can I drop you off?" I said, intending to take him to the course boundary as quickly as possible. "Thanks, no." And there it was, folks, completely outfoxed by an old coot.

Every few days the offer got the same, "No thanks." I was feeling like Ricky Nelson in *Rio Bravo*—not a boy, but not a man yet, either. And this mongoose was making off with all the wild eggs!

"What should we do about that old guy poaching golf balls?" I asked one morning. Ruley looked up from his hash browns, didn't stop chewing. Eventually . . . "Wears a hat and sunglasses?"

"Yeah. I tried to give him the hint, but he keeps coming back."

For about a minute, everybody looked at everybody, then Ruley stood up, picking up only his own check. The others did the same. A line entered my head. "What do you mean, *we*, kemosabe?"

It probably was a coincidence, but that day my game piece was a shovel. My partner's job that day was to keep the truckbed loaded with sand, smoke, and cigarettes, and watch me from a stool at the hot dog stand. We didn't know it then, but I'm an artist now. And a day of shoveling could have robbed me and the world of my hands' softness.

Toward evening, my hands caked with blood, caked with sweat, anyway, a voice from a cloud told me that the little old man I'd been harassing took the firemen to the racetrack once a year—via limousine—and left the car in "preferred parking, which is right in front."

Ruley was a kind, fatherly, strong boss. And he had lived long enough that nothing masculine surprised him. In a bad heat wave, you'd work through the night to save the greens, moving the sprinklers by hand. But a previous social engagement couldn't be canceled; it wouldn't be right. And so, with Goddess as my copilot, I'd do that late shift while she had a couple of quarts. The greens would be as soft and tender as beer-soaked lips. Maybe Ruley didn't know, but I was more cheerful working double shifts than single ones.

The National College of Education had dorms on one side of the golf course, and classrooms on the other, with sweet grass and plenty of water in between. Summer school brought a cattle drive of women to the golf course. Soon I'd cut me a blue-ribbon heifer out of the herd.

I had to arrange my work schedule to encounter the migration as many times as possible in the course of the day, while remaining casual. I would cut greens out of sequence—nine, eight, five, three—in order to appear miraculously everywhere, anywhere. I would wait in the narrow tunnel that passed under the El tracks in the dark. Undetected and unexpected. For how long? And what was I thinking?

Finally I'd hear voices coming into the tunnel. After the eyes adjusted, a whoop. "Oh my God, who's that?" I'd be sipping a root beer, my mind a million miles away, until I'd notice them. I'd notice them passing by on either side of me, about a foot away. Then the look: "What? You've never seen someone dark, mysterious, and caked with sweat on a five?" They'd leave the tunnel, I'd blast out the other side, barrel along surface streets, reenter the golf course, back up to a left-uncut green, offload my mower, and be half-finished by the time the stampede passed by.

When you think about it, how easily I could have become a stalker. But that's not the look I have in my eyes out there now . . . I'm just imagining what it would have been like to have a summer job at Pebble Beach.

There will be fifty or sixty thousand people out here today. Before most of them arrive, I'm going out for a run. Some of my more challenging ensembles could work if the top button of my trousers were secured. It has been my observation that a number of golfers experiencing turnaround years had recently embarked on workout regimens.

My gear includes tight-fitting athletic pants of the kind I would never wear. Tragically, I'm recognized by a dude teeing off at the new par-three fifth hole. He cracked me on my ballet look. All I can do is enjoy his long iron's squirm through the marine layer, with no chance of a dance. Hit the six-wood, Harry.

Summoning all the athletic ability worth risking, I jump over the ropes and onto the course. Steve McQueen in *The Great Escape*. Theme music pounding in my ears. The greenkeepers look up as I roll by, then turn away. The bandana covering my head and large glasses give me a postoperative elective cosmetic surgery look. It's a look I favor, a look that says, "Don't look twice."

Inside the ropes it's safe, but the gallery is where the fun is. Like the zoo. The closer you get to the bars, the more interesting the animals. It's hard to be sure which side of the rope holds the animals, but fair to say there is wildlife on both sides.

Okay, what if I'm wrong and guess the rope is working for me. I could end up jelly side up or jelly side down. The smart move is to respect the ocean. That's one thing I learned from the surfers. These guys could swim out into waves I could not approach without an outboard, but they had nothing but respect for big blue. You could ride it all day, but anytime it felt the urge, you were finished.

The crowd is where the fun is. Of course, the better
golf you play, the more fun they have. If you can recover
from deep in the trees or from within the gallery, you
have the makings of golf excitement. Arnie, Seve, and
me, in order of ability. With them, you can never rule out
the possibility of a birdie. With me, the possibility of a
par, a bogey, or one of the most exciting moments in
pro-am golf, a net par.

Alone, I'm fine. A few years ago, associating with a
gallery member, I got in trouble and was told in no
uncertain terms to stay within the ropes. I argued that I
can't keep my ball within the ropes, and if I played a
provisional ball all day long, that wouldn't be golf any-
more.

I was told it was a safety issue.

"C'mon, you let Gerald Ford play; you don't care that
much about safety."

"It's your safety that's our concern."

"An assassin? If he wants me, he'll get me."

"Nonetheless, you'll be safer if you stay within the
ropes."

It was about crowd control, they said. Crowd control
is my business. I have a highly developed sense of a
crowd, and whether or not they need attention.

This year our path encountered some of this nation's
young people, out for a good time at the golf tourna-

ment. Unbeknownst to them, someone had put alcohol in their beer, and this had obviously happened several hours ago. Apparently they had gotten separated from the sitter or aunt or uncle in charge.

Their cries for help were rowdy and offensive, but hey, they cried for help. As a responsible adult, I offered them my suggestions, but I already had responsibilities. What they needed was someone with whom they could spend quality time. Preferably someone in a red marshal's jacket with a walkie-talkie.

Some crowds need more control than others. I was there at Shinnecock in 1986, a difficult course to play and an extremely difficult course to walk. Which to this, let's just call them a New York crowd, was probably very irritating. New York City at its most heartwarming is a death dance twixt vehicles and pedestrians. Put these same walkers on a stretch of windswept dunes, with wide USGA-enforced detours, and you've got a recipe for circumambient crankiness.

The players get to walk straight lines from tee to green. So who died and left them kings? That's a vibe that's out there. I almost said *the* vibe, but it's just a vibe to be aware of: Get a load of the big shot. And in a group, New Yorkers expect more show-me than do Missourians.

For example, the Yankees versus the Seattle Mariners

in the 1995 playoffs. Many more power ties than the normal box seat crowd—the cannibals fresh from Wall Street, having skipped lunch, and here's the catch of the day, flown in fresh from the Pacific Northwest.

Heavy fan abuse, or interest perhaps. Regardless, an explicit intent to surpass ordinary home-field advantage. Yet one voice, trading-pit-trained, cut through the night to the on-deck circle.

"Hey, Cora, take three strikes and sit down!"

"Buhner, why did you come back? We traded you so we'd never have to look at you again. Get your weak act out of here!"

These Mariners were not used to this kind of sweet-talking, and they never raised their gaze from the sod. They didn't wave their bats much, either, self-esteem being quite low by the time each reached the batter's box.

Then Ken Griffey, Jr., stepped from the dugout.

"Junior, who the hell are you kidding? You got a very nice career going out there in that podunk bandbox you call a stadium in Seattle, but you wouldn't have fifteen home runs in this ballpark, Junior."

Griffey, unlike the other Mariners, stares right back at the voice, a smile on his face.

"You've had a great run out there in Little League,

Griffey, but you can't play here. Your dad couldn't play here, either. We ran him out of town."

Griffey keeps staring back, still smiling. This one-sided conversation is amusing and engrossing the first forty rows of boxes.

"You got a beautiful smile there, son. But you can't play at this level. Didn't Piniella tell you?"

The crowd has laughed at some of this; partly entertained and partly embarrassed. Griffey interrupts his smile. It's his turn to bat.

A pitch comes over the plate at the belt, and the horsehide starts singing Sinatra's "New York, New York" in a very high key. Big-time. About one point five seconds later, the ball lands somewhere in the upper deck. We all watch Griffey's home run trot. It's a pretty good one. He's been practicing. He dents home plate, slaps a few hands on his way back, and is just about to disappear into the dugout when his childlike face registers, "Oh, I almost forgot something." He searches the boxes for the face that goes with the voice and ambidexterously flips a batting-gloved bird straight at the guy. Junior obviously wants to be a part of New York, New York.

Griffey's next trip to the on-deck circle was met with: "Hey Junior, take it easy on me. What? You trying to kill me? You're making me look bad here. C'mon, go easy, fella. It's just a game."

The crowd enjoyed this very much, but nowhere as much as Griffey's salute. This at-bat was not eventful; all was quiet on the Eastern front.

But life is full of mystery. And if you've ever seen Gunther Gebel Williams of the Ringling Bros., Barnum & Bailey Circus in a swimsuit, you must ask the question, "Why did he continue after the first time he was mauled?"

You see, Griffey has returned to the on-deck circle, and once again the voice has risen from the boxes.

"Hey, Mr. Lucky. Yeah, you, Junior. It only opens once, my friend. You got your miracle for the year. Count your blessings when you go to sleep tonight. Three strikes lookin', amigo, you've blown your wad. Remember to say thanks."

I don't remember whether it was the first pitch or the second, but it was the last. There's some kind of alley out in right-center field. If you hit it far enough back there, they say you can ride with the conductor of the D train. Well, I think the conductor let Griffey wear his hat and pull the horn.

This trot was better, because he'd had more practice. It seemed to take longer, perhaps because many hundred people were switching allegiance, removing hats, and turning jackets inside out. Once again Griffey dented home plate, hand-slapped his way back, and once again in beatific afterthought awarded the international badge of suggested self-love. Simply breathtaking.

What remarkable power of transformation. This extraordinary athlete had turned abuse into high-octane fuel that lifted that little Haitian Sputnik free of our atmosphere. Delightfully, athletically, and emotionally instructive.

Griffey has mastered his game. Like Greg Norman has mastered his. But that day on Long Island, when a fan lobbed some grief at Greg Norman after a less than perfect shot, the Australian reared back and winged a verbal boomerang right back.

I got a very sick feeling in my stomach, as did friends around me. His retort did not slay his attacker, nor organize a posse. Instead, it awakened sleeping jackals in the crowd. This menacing new head count swayed the herd to give up the shark to natural selection.

The next few holes were pretty tough to take.

Did you ever see *Gallipoli*? It's a Peter Weir film, a true story of a suicidal hill charge by Australian infantrymen. This is not pick-on-Australia day, it really is a great film, and it popped into my head when I thought of the futility of Greg's counterattack. But while you're at it, if you're going to rent *Gallipoli*, you should also pick up *Zulu* with a young Michael Caine. It, too, must be seen.

Back to the golf ugliness. There was blood in the water now and any tiny error of Greg's was met with snorts and cackles. The pack's surly passage swelled with drifters looking for a free meal. It was open season on Norman and he was angry. From a hillock greenside, his baiter lured him into another exchange. Did Greg really say, "If you have something to say, save it for later when I can reply." I think so. I think that's what he said.

I certainly understood the impulse. I've had it. When the overserved young people howled at our foursome this week, it was five holes before I could play golf again. A violated rage prevents you from playing well. Suddenly you mistrust everybody, you're embarrassed and angry that you have lost your cool. That's me, and I wasn't playing for the U.S. Open.

Greg Norman was the best player in the world at that time. He was in every major. He was in the middle of a spectacular run of snakebit second-place finishes that can happen only if you are the number-one player in the world. Dominant may be too strong, but superior might not be. A decade later, galleries would show him enormous compassion after his Masters meltdown. Once again—what's more impressive, that he shot a 78 at Augusta on Sunday or that after three rounds he led The Masters by six strokes?

I once played nine holes with Greg at Grand Cypress. He has an Aussie accent, but I had no trouble understanding because he kept repeating himself: "Bill, I think yaw bawl went in about 'ere."

Sure, we collapse . . . but we fight back.

He was a good shepherd that day, hacking through the sawgrass in search of the one that was lost. That day he hit five of the best golf shots I'd ever seen, out of tens of thousands that I have seen. I never saw anybody hit it better.

Since then he's made more money than Murdoch. He's also taken on the PGA Tour, which I can understand, and gotten hurt partying with Clinton, which we as a nation understand. And at the Presidents' Cup Down Under, he was observed having fun with the home continent crowd.

Earlier this year I had kind of a . . . social problem and I knew I had to make nice. It occurred to me to simply say, "Hey, let's not make it so long. We need to spend some personal time together, my friend. No business. This is nuts. We definitely gotta do a lunch."

But I couldn't. I just couldn't. Not because I was too hip, or not capable of workmanlike insincerity. I can lie; God, anybody who can lie to himself like I can, rocks my world with his falsity.

No, I just found something better to say. I picked it up in an elevator.

"I'd love to get you out to Sweet Gum. Because you love golf, don't you? We've got a new green superintendent who really knows watering. I should get you out there for our member-guest, because you really love golf, don't you?"

* * *

I took a job this year on what we call an "art movie." It turns out that not all movies are art movies, so the ones that are need to be labeled. For everyone's safety.

"Yeah, but how do you know?"

Good question. Let's define an art movie:

art mo-vie \'art 'mu-ve\ n.(1926): 1 a motion picture with little or no chance of commercial success 2 a motion picture in which the actors performing are paid the federal minimum wage 3 a motion picture cast with actors not desired in motion pictures with a chance of commercial success, esp. those in drug or alcohol rehabilitation, or those with multiple recent failures 4 a motion picture in which the cast and crew is worked to physical exhaustion in the name of art 5 a motion picture characterized by lengthy suspension of actual work while waiting for art to occur syn see DEATH SHIP

6 obs. a powerful motion picture which easily and skillfully demonstrates an understanding of the rules and ideas necessary to practice the profession of moviemaking; a film: ART FILM—v. to drive a cast or crew member insane by use of low wages and artful procrastination.

Now you're up to speed. Once upon a time, on David Letterman's show promoting what turned out to be an art movie, I was asked by Dave if the Academy of Motion Picture Arts and Sciences might be recognizing my work in this art film. And I told that late-night Louie that my thinking was I'd win an Oscar the same year I won the Heisman Trophy.

Days later I received a script with a handwritten note.

> Bill,
> This is your Heisman.
> Yours,
> Tim Robbins

You can imagine what this means to a guy with two years of eligibility remaining. Plus, the script is ambitious on the level of Citizen Kane; it even reads and feels like it. Which makes it—who in this class has been following?—an art movie.

My reaction can only be described as "Alamo, huh? Hmmm . . . sounds good. Where do I sign up?"

I must have been very vulnerable. I took the bad money, hours, and working conditions finding this upside: At least it won't turn out to be an art movie. Change the title to *Hell's Snowball.* The whole world would be on the same page.

Tim lured quite a number of moths to this campfire. Vanessa Redgrave, sorry, art film. Must use alphabetical billing: Hank Azaria, Bill Murray, Rube Blades, Joan Cusack, John Cusack, Cary Elwes, Susan Sarandon, John Turturro, Emily Watson. Now it may not read like Andersonville, but not one of them will ever tell the true story of what happened. *The Abyss* without the budget.

Surrounded by unselfish craftsmen and women, I still have an actor's desire to be treated like Elizabeth Taylor. Just special, that's all. Surprise me in the morning, with little thoughtfuls: silk scarf, forced narcissus bulbs, a zircon. May my hope chest fill, and then just one more thing, Lord. Teach me to forget the meaning of the word "late."

When I do schlock with other hacks, I come late, in order to hold up hundreds of people for hours, days, and weeks. This is how one earns respect.

But on an art movie . . . well, there's a reason Elizabeth Taylor doesn't do art movies. Try as you may, you can't show up late. Every day turns out to be the day they decided to paint the chapel ceiling.

"Signor Buonarroti, I was hoping to invite some people over for mass and a rosary . . . Are you almost finished?"

"I'm going for something here, Your Holiness. Tell you what. Bring in the College of Cardinals so I can take a look at them from up here, then you guys can go to lunch while I do some touch-ups."

A few summers back, Billy and I got together for a little family golf, up at a nondescript course resort course in Wisconsin, the name of which I can't remember. Billy wasn't playing too well—his mind didn't seem to be into the game. Meanwhile, I'd found a rich vein of form—well over my head—and I was drilling him. At the seventeenth green, I beat him, two and one. So as we walk to eighteen, a long dogleg par-four, he says "Whaddaya say, double or nothing?" I take the bet, then knock a nice tee shot up the middle. Billy hits it OB, then drops another ball and pushes it into a miniforest. But then we round the corner of the dogleg and realize someone has let the word out—a hundred people are waiting for us at the green. Bill's eyes immediately light up. He hunkers down to his ball and rips a knee-high two-iron through the branches. It runs all the way to the green, finishing about thirty feet from the hole. I, who have never played in front of such a crowd, gag. My approach snipes into some rough, I skull my third into a greenside bunker, skull my fourth back across the green into another bunker, then skull on and three-putt for an eight. Brother Billy, loving every minute of this, milks his pre-putt routine for a couple of minutes and then drains the thirty-footer for a crowd-enrapturing five.

—*Brian Doyle-Murray*

(Christine Lesniak)

If you can't make 'em wait, that's really taking a big club out of the bag. But then, sometimes you catch a break.

I had been spotted at a televised basketball game. The production erroneously thought this explained my strange pattern of availability dates—that if the Chicago Bulls were playing, I would be unavailable to work. But if they'd bothered to check my contract, they'd have found I had no Jack Nicholson clause!

When my director, Mr. Robbins, told me over personally shaken martinis and one of his Cubans . . . that there was a schedule problem—a theater location was available only on a certain day that another of the actors was available, and so on—I fixed him with a fish-eye smile.

He thought it was an NBA line in the sand, but it was only a whisper in my ear: "Vermouth." Then Tim did something very unusual, for him. He panicked.

"Perhaps we could get a TV on the set."

You could have heard a pin drop.

"That way we wouldn't miss the game."

Tim is a man's man, whatever that means to you: Robert Mitchum, Ian McKellen, Ru Paul. Tim enjoys sports and actually plays them. But that TV wasn't coming in for him. He was bringing it in to get the work done. Television. Work. Television. Work. Hmmmm.

The set was a dressing room in the wings of an old vaudeville house on the Jersey side of the river. It was tight and dressed with mirrors, which made for difficult shooting. If a camera and operator are seen on film in the reflection of one of the mirrors, that cameraman will have seven years of bad luck.

Which makes for some fun when, in the middle of a take, the camera operator speaks—you see, he has no lines in the script.

"I'm sorry, I'm going to have to cut. I see myself."

"As others see you?"

"Back to one, everybody."

Then follows the mildly embarrassed silence as the camera on its dolly mount rolls back to the starting position. This silence is just scrumptious after ten or fifteen botched takes. Not all miscues are camera, but they may as well be, 'cause they're the only ones moving. The camera on a dolly is a three-headed monster: the dolly grip pushing a camera on big rubber wheels; the first camera assistant walking beside, pulling focus; the operator astride his platform seat.

Tim Robbins, a script supervisor wearing headphones, and the director of photography huddle in front of a video monitor that shows the frame that the film camera is capturing. A sound camera with a large boom mike and the second camera assistant, who smacks the sticks together to slate each scene, crowd into this not very large space.

It's hot, it's claustrophobic, and the camera keeps breaking the fourth wall. About an hour into this, you start thinking, "Couldn't we maybe put a ship in a bottle instead?"

Out on the theater's stage, there's a party going on. Plenty of fresh air, a cooler of drinks instead of the camera monitor; a long cable run in from the street leads to a large television showing the National Basketball Association playoff finals.

So you could do a take of the scene, they'd cut for technical reasons, and while they'd roll back and forth, trying to solve the problem, I could go watch the game. I'd figured out my own route in and out of the dressing room: through a back door, that led to a fire exit. It was not a desired route, winding its way in darkness over spaghetti bowls of electrical cable, occasionally awakening a worker who thought he'd found his niche.

The mirrors caused so much trouble that my yo-yoing slipped underneath the radar. Solutions start with "I'll just lean my head back." Next the camera crew dons velour blackout suits, complete with cowls. This is always good for self-control—someone you work a few feet from all day is now dressed as a satanic priest. I can ignore a prominent fever blister, but I feel the need to look deeply into the eyes of this cohort.

These visiting Muppets contribute to a breakdown of law and order. The mirror solutions near this stage: "My head is aching, I'd better cut it off."

Every cinematic crisis can be defused with a spray can: WD-40, enamel paint, Evian Actress Atomizer, dulling spray, hair spray, RV commode disinfectant and deodorizer, Binaca, Windex, 409, foam fire retardant, ether, and, when mirrors reflect—snowy stuff.

Have you ever seen how a thickly bearded drag queen applies makeup? First, early stages of denial with just a hint of base and a touch of rouge; then a fearful hint of reality, and the change from Chinese sculpting brushes to four-inch Latex; finally, deciding on the open casket House of Wax look favored by Moloney and Sons.

Snowy stuff is applied in the same way. My face in the mirror first has a glistening glow. Then it's an agar-facial-in-progress; then fallen-through-ice-fishing-trapped-beneath-the-surface-save-me!; finally there's so much snowy stuff that it could be me in the looking glass, or it could be the Sasquatch. It has, however, circumscribed the acting assignment for me. I simply must portray a character with multiple cataracts.

This is all business as usual, even nicer. Usually when this many attempts are required the action involves danger, discomfort, toxicity, or full-frontal nudity. The only horror here is right there in the mirror.

All this fun has taken us three and a half quarters into the game, and I'm now spending more time on the stage than on the set. The fiddling continues between takes and when we're ready to try again, the cry goes up: "Ready for first team."

To differentiate from a stand-in or second team calling out. This cry is heard and repeated by every assistant director, production assistant, and little suck within the sound of the first assistant director's voice. And since his voice is broadcast over walkie-talkie, to the A.D.'s, P.A.'s, and L.S.'s, some wearing their walkies on their belts, it's a sensurround experience.

After a while of this, Tim comes to the stage, the decision made to watch the last five minutes of the game. Any mother with dinner on the table knows how long the last five minutes of an NBA game can last. Did you guess thirty-five minutes?

The clock stops every time there is an infraction. The clock stops every time the ball goes out of bounds. The clock stops every time there is a foul. The clock also stops for timeouts. Some of the timeouts are twenty seconds, and some are for a minute, and sometimes when the timeouts are for a minute, the network decides to tell us about a very special "Third Rock from the Sun" and sell some pickups and beer. And sometimes you hear Bob Costas's voice say, "Now Phil Jackson has changed that twenty-second timeout to a full timeout. When we come back for the final one minute and nineteen seconds, Chicago leads Utah by only one point."

Every time we left the game to talk beer, pickups, or a very special "Third Rock," the theme music for the NBA would come up. Loudly, jauntily, and very un-art-movie-like. You'd hear a grunt and the jaw of Tim Robbins, Directors' Guild of America, would tighten just a bit more. I felt for him, but hey, ya buys the ticket and youse takes the ride.

Well, it was fun while it lasted, basking in that glow that can only come from a crew that is not working. It was a good game, too; close, hard-fought, epic, and ultimately, tied at the end of regulation.

Yep, overtime.

But first, beer, pickups, and a very special, must-see you know what. As the NBA on NBC theme music swelled, I recognized the look on Robbins's face. I'd seen it on the face of a visitor to New York as he learned how to play three-card monte.

Tim was in a lot of pain, so we tried to work during the overtime. I was very bad and walked to the TV at the end of each take. We'd do that "Ready for first team!" dance and try another. They should have put a leash on me; I couldn't help myself. Finally, Tim marched in from the set, his shoes pounding a warning rhythm of "I HAVE HAD ENOUGH," punched through the crowd, and like the daddy home from bowling, snapped off the game.

Several comments did not occur to me.

"Oh no you don't."

"We did all our homework."

"You're kidding, aren't you?"

"You don't have to watch. We'll watch and tell you what happens."

"There's only two minutes left."

What I did say was "Oh, Tim, you were doing so well . . ."

We finished soon after, and soon after that, I finished shooting on the film. I greatly appreciated how hard Tim had worked on the film, as well as his heroic attempt to watch an NBA finals game while Disney was paying us. I wanted to let him know it was all okay. Somehow I thought a round of country club golf might do the trick. Gee, I knew this story was about golf.

Tim Robbins is not a candidate for golf club membership. He's tall, he believes in equal rights for men and women, that Haitians shouldn't be jailed at Guantanamo for testing positive, that political prisoners shouldn't be tortured, and that spinach served in the club dining room should be free-range.

Tim brought his brother David, a fine musician who did the movie's score. And I invited my friend Ahmad, who brought cigars. David and I walked so they could smoke cigars in peace. I hoped by partnering with Tim, it would show I forgave him for what he'd done.

The guy has a frightening golf swing, but ice hockey taught him the concept of shots on goal. It was a wonderful round and a wonderful day. It felt great to see the man who once was my boss getting a break from the grind. He still had another ten months of work ahead before the film would be finished. Movie directors work so much harder than actors; it's no wonder they get paid less.

Which was little consolation, down one with two to play. The final two holes at my course aren't easy. One has a tricky green and the other is downright hard. And our opponents were conversationally inept, often returning to the status of the match. Toss in a little sibling rivalry and you have significance.

My partner parred the last two holes and we won the match. He had to go directly to a sound recording session at work and left almost immediately. He wouldn't play golf again till the following spring. But he'd pulled victory out of a hat like a vaudeville magician. I guess that bodes well for the film, too.

Sunday

My eldest brother, Ed, was a dedicated caddy, even winning a Chick Evans Caddy Scholarship to Northwestern, which would make him a wildcat. At dinner each night, he would spellbind us with stories of fine gentlemen whose clubs he'd carried. Genghis Khan didn't do as well by Marco Polo.

If my kid encored arias about any club member—even a lucky sperm club member—that child would be tenderly wrapped in swaddling clothes that very night, and left on the guy's doorstep with a note: PLEASE RAISE HIM, AS WE THINK ONLY YOU CAN.

My father never asked, as my sister Peggy had, "Edward, does this mean you're leaving?" But years later, Dad did leave gold-mine shares intended for Edward to me.

One year Ed caddied for this guy who had a real shot at winning the club championship. He idolized this guy, and the buildup was weeks. "Joe was stripin' it today— four-iron 205"—and my parents, to their credit, let him go on . . . "Oh, isn't that nice . . ." Me, I felt like saying, "Ed, wait a minute. You've got me mixed up."

"'Mixed up'?"

"Yeah, you've got me mixed up with someone who cares."

Anyway his guy loses in the final, and it's a terrible thing. Ed tells the guy he feels his pain, then invites him to our house for a sorrows-drowning drink. Invites him to our house!!!?

No one ever came to our house—at least not without warning us. Our house was a wreck, a constant, claustrophobic mess. (To this day, all of my siblings have a problem with neatness.) It was a place to set out from, not to entertain—especially not one of the members of Indian Hill.

We had these cousins from the city—the Heisers— who used to show up at our house unannounced a couple times a year. They'd take a Sunday drive and pop in on us. There'd be a still Sunday afternoon and suddenly one of the kids would spot the car. It was like Ishmael spotting the Great White Whale.

A cry would go out: "Oh my God, the Heisers are here!"

That signaled a mass frenzy as the entire family tore into action, running in every direction while picking up as much stuff as we could hold—sort of a reverse Supermarket Sweep, where everything went back onto the shelves. Closets were jammed, clothes were stuffed under couches, and shirts were tucked in just in time for Mom to open the door with a big smile and an "Jean? How *nice* to see you."

It was such a nightmare that we'd occasionally pull it on my mother even when they weren't there. Just to send her into a panic, one of us would look out the window and say, "Oh, great. The Heisers are here."

So anytime someone was headed to our house, it was a surreal situation. Somebody's coming!!!

So Ed calls and says, "I'm bringing this guy over for a drink."

A drink? In our house? So we had to scramble.

My dad was a real gent, he made him a drink—and so was this guy—but it was very uncomfortable all around. Not unlike Ty Webb's visit to Carl Spackler's house.

Ed always really liked golf club members. He left caddying to work in the pro shop, just to be nearer them. The family now believes some of Ed's ailments may have been spread by contagious Indian Hill members. Let's examine the life of one of the more virulent viruses.

This scene got cut, but I'll never forget filming it. Bill and I were squeezed together on the seat of one of those wide greens mowers, the kind with the sets of blades that lift up on each side. Since Billy was to drive, I sort of scrunched in beside him, half on the seat and half off. "Watch the way you drive this thing," I told him. "Those blades look pretty sharp and I don't want to fall off." Silly me—that was all the invitation he needed. He threw the thing into gear, took a hard right turn, and before I knew it I was on the ground. I rolled out of the way just in time to see the blades zip within an inch of my ass.

—*Chevy Chase*

Disturbed member finishes round, finds no cronies in clubhouse. Realizes clubhouse attendant, bartender, and waiters are not golfers, either. Enters pro shop. There finds eager-beaver employee/golfer, would-be member. Phage attaches to my brother's brain, replicates.

Preventable, perhaps. More probably, inevitable.

You say, what happened? My God, that could have stricken my spouse, or even my child! How would I know? What should I look for? We have one piece of luck. The pure strain is observable in my brother Edward.

"Hey, Ed, it's me, Billy. How are you doing?"

"Pretty good. I played golf yesterday."

". . . Uh, yeah. How'd you do?"

"Well, I get to fifteen, and I'm one over. I hit it way right, where I couldn't get home from. So I figure, I'll just hit five-iron, leave myself another five-iron, have a chance for birdie."

"Sure."

"I just try to hit a cut shot, but I don't make a full turn, grip goes soft on me, and I put it in the pond. Take a drop, figure knock it on with a wood, maybe make a putt, save par."

"Sure. It's all you can do at that point."

"It's all I can do. I got two-twenty uphill, so I try to kill it."

"Oh, no. You yank it. Hold on a second. I have to do something."

"It catches the last limb on the last tree on the left. Knocks around in it, I'm praying maybe it'll kick it out—nothing. Four feet farther and it would have hit the side of the hill, kicked down onto the green. I get up there, it's stymied at the base of the trunk; I gotta chip out. I go with the flop wedge, but I hit it fat, leave myself nine feet. I miss the putt—snowman.

"I'm walkin' to the tee, thinkin', 'Okay, par in for seventy-six. Maybe make a birdie, seventy-five, my best round since March.' I take out my driver. I don't know why. I usually hit three-wood there; knock a two-iron on the green and take my par. But I figure, 'Aah, get the birdie first—then I just gotta go par-par.' I pure it, but right. Catch a break, it's in, but the OB stake is in my backswing, and you can't move it. I'm concentrating so hard on taking it back inside, I push it right past the birdhouse underneath the cherry trees. It's soaking wet over there, I hit a miracle shot from my knees about ten yards short of the green. We're all laughing about how wet my pants are. I get over the ball, it's all I can think about, I chili-dip it into the bunker. So I sink for bogey, right? But I don't. It hangs on the lip. Double.

"Now I'm wet and I'm mad. We'd been killing these guys. Tied the front, had them four down on the back;

and they'd pressed. Had them two down on the press and they'd pressed again, and we took it. All of a sudden, we're only two up on the back, even on the first press, and two down on the second press. I get cocky and press them back and they gotta take it, 'cause we took theirs, right? They *have* to take it. We didn't *have* to take their push but we did. So . . . We play with these guys all the time.

"Well, this one guy, he sells radio time for a rock station. And those guys know the raunchiest jokes of anybody. He tells a joke about Diana Ross and the guy, you know this guy, he had a show, then they went off, they had a big final-episode show—now he's back on, he's got his own show. I can see his face. Oh, what's his name! You know this guy. It'll come to me. He tells a story about the two of them like it's a true story, and you get sucked in—neither of them is on . . . he's over, the other's in the bunker. So at the punch line, you realize it's really not a true story, it's a racist, shock ending. I didn't like the joke, but you can't help laughing. I would not repeat this joke. But that may have been the point of the joke. You would know better than I. So I'm thinking about all this, hit it in the water, chip up, and make bogey. Then the one guy gets up and down, with a stroke. He hadn't done anything all day."

"I'm sorry, Ed, my little guy was out there alone on his bike, talking to the UPS driver. Thought the guy was Santa Claus."

"Huh? . . . Oh. Oh . . . have you been playing at all?"

"Some. Hittin' it good, but I need to putt a little better."

"Yeah. You putt for dough."

"Yep."

"Okay, brother, you take it easy. I'll talk to you soon."

"You, too, bro. Toodle-oo."

I can hear you thinking, "Why have you shown us this? To frighten us? What have we learned about this virus?" Two important things. It doesn't make you a bad person. And it isn't contagious over the phone. There's no reason to think we won't find a cure.

On the other hand, it was Ed who provided material for the central character in *Caddyshack*. Greatest golf film ever made. Arguably the greatest film ever made, although perhaps that's a drunken argument.

The film is really the gripping tale of the Murray brothers' first experiments with employment. It suited us. You didn't have to punch a clock; that failure would come later. No dress code; you could work barefoot. No age limit, no income tax. I want this job now!

There were Three Musketeers of *Caddyshack*. First, my brother Brian, who made my career possible, wrote a comic parable of a pauper who'd be prince. He wrote the events of his and my brother Ed's caddy life in a way that showed he'd paid attention—and had fun doing it. He may not out-live us all, but he's had the most fun. Harold Ramis's achievement in directing the film was the melodic blend of several different comic styles. Think of the players—Chevy Chase, Rodney Dangerfield, Ted Knight, Sara Holcombe, Brian Doyle-Murray, Michael O'Keefe, Bill Murray, Cindy Morgan . . . We're not even in the same Rolodex. It was a much harder task than people appreciate.

And Doug Kenney, may he rest in peace. When he died at thirty-three, a playful planet fell from the sky. His dad Harry, a country-club tennis pro, and Doug brought that history to the movie. Doug was also a creator of *National Lampoon,* became a millionaire, and tried to give it all away. He picked up every check he ever saw. He had a Village apartment he left unlocked. If you needed to take a leak or a nap, or read a book in the afternoon, it was there. And, when he came home, he was happy to see you there. The mystical Zen approach of Chevy's charac-ter was Doug's contribution. He had an idea for a putter with electromagnetic sensors that would signal you to putt when you'd reached alpha state. Kenny encouraged everybody, helped everybody, was just a great big little boy who wished to be amazed. I think *Caddyshack* will probably live as long as Doug Kenney's spirit is alive.

* * *

The Cinderella story scene was a spur-of-the-moment idea. "Get me some flowers," I said. "Four rows of mums."

They still weren't sure where I was going. But the main idea was to cut down flowers. See, there is a weird thing that greenkeepers can't help but have that was a factor in Carl's persona: the anger over the class tension. (You see it in other parts of the movie, too—the shoe guy grinding the club members' shoes down.) Anyone in the service area has had this potential for anger—and therein was the impetus. Carl, right in front of the pro shop, randomly off his rocker.

The golf swing part was absolute joy. Never wrote a word of script. It just came from my head into the camera. I did it in one take—but I knew it had worked. I just knew where I was—I was comin' down the home stretch. It's the same feeling we all have on our golf courses, playing alone, we become the narrator inside our minds. Or when we play putting games: "This one, then, for the Open." I think that's one of the appeals of the movie—the Walter Mitty aspect that every golfer goes through.

The gopher thing just sort of evolved, too. At one point they just said, "Any ideas?" That day I went to the greenkeeper's shack—the actual greenkeeper's shack—and saw the fertilizer. "Let's make a bunker," I said, and the set director got it right away. "And let's make some explosives out of clay." I just sort of walked around the shack for fifteen minutes and it started jumping into my head. Maybe it was the fertilizer.

I thought there should be a whole bizarre world for this guy. So I went out and designed this foxhole with bags of fertilizer as bulkheading. I thought he should be carving plastic explosives—varmint Cong, the thing with the scope—that stuff. (They bomb gophers, don't they?) We shot the scene the next day.

Yes, as a caddy you learned how to smoke, curse, play cards. But more importantly, *when* to. I don't know many caddies that turned out bad. The gig was a primer of social conduct lessons.

First, manners: Sir, ma'am. Please, thank you, you're welcome. I think the most reliable determinant of a person's worth is manners. Nowadays, I meet many more people than I have time to accurately plumb. No manners, *no màs tiempo, señor.*

The job also develops a service personality. Not indentured or slavish, but capable of putting another person's needs first. Do you know what I mean? If you are sick, if you're in trouble, out of your element, someone with more than just kindness is needed—someone Samaritan. Someone with the ability to do for another what needs to be done.

They say you can tell a lot about a person by the way he treats a waiter. Or a caddy, you might add. It's the manners and ease with which one accepts being served. Those who can't serve graciously can't be graciously served. This is more easily learned from service.

Finally, the forgotten virtue of tact. A caddy knows exactly how good a player is. He sees the potential, he sees the coordination and the behavior of the player through good golf and bad. Yet you don't hear "You're slamming that club back in the bag because you hit out of bounds. Aren't you, sir?"

It's a caddy point of pride to be succinct. On a good day, I could go an entire round and say only "Nice shot" and "You're away, sir." There was a cool to it, a respect for the silences of the walking game.

I remember one afternoon a long time ago, when I was still a single caddy. It was a late loop, the sun was low in the West; we'd only be playing nine. Mr. Marquis Bowman, a long hitter for a man of advanced age, had hit the green with his third shot at the par-five first. He took his putter and quickly strode ahead as I dropped the bag en route to the next tee. His alacrity proved to have been caused by discomfort. As he neared the green, he began to backfire, gripping his Spalding Cash-In more tightly. Finally, a soundless Vesuvian eruption accompanied by a light show.

You heard me. Floating in the wake of Mr. Bowman were large multicolored gas bubbles of blue, purple, and amber. They had the life expectancy of soap bubbles blown from a bottle, and they popped in the same way, into droplets. It didn't last a long time.

Where, you might ask, is the tact? Where is the secret shared between golfer and caddy? The understood confidence that what happens on the golf course remains on the golf course?

You think this is easy, to tell this story? And what does it mean in the arc of this book? What's being served here? May I get in a word edgewise?

First of all, I have kept this story in my bosom for thirty-five years. This secret lived longer than some of my friends. Longer than Jesus, or Otis Redding. I would rather have any of them back than that secret. Hester Prynne gave it up sooner than I did.

Is Mr. Bowman alive? I hope so, God bless his long life. He's certainly learned to laugh at the little things. If he's gone, may he rest in peace, with a prayer that his leaving was not caused by complications from the condition first noticed but unreported three and a half decades ago.

This has been tough. But once again, the French have an expression—better remorse than regret. By telling this true tale, I hope to show the length and breadth of tact that is possible in a young man taught in concert with manners and service. The boy caddying for you today could die with your secret. If he doesn't end up writing a book about it.

My most recent favorite round of golf was in the club championship. Well, flight championship, with a gent named Ed Kobacker. Wary of Ed as an opponent—he smoked thin cigars and wore an Australian sun hat—I was almost rattled. It turned out, though, that he just liked thin cigars, and his hat. We had eighteen holes of the nicest, most civilized conversation—about family, and vacations, and living. Never once talked about golf or the match except to say "nice shot."

It reminded me of peaceful times as a caddy when I would listen to players carry on such a conversation. A child seen and not heard. Here it was, decades later, the same courteous conversation in walking rhythm, and the elegant sensation when in the presence of someone comfortable in his own skin.

Every golf life has seen the game's sleight-of-hand. Not the vagary of the ball's bounce, or the miraculous appearance of practice-tee form, but some round or outing when golf made it possible to see the larger, and see oneself as a player in the big game everyone is playing.

There are some things that are just not acceptable at all. There are some things that are just not acceptable at all that take place on the golf course. Some of the things that take place on the golf course that are just not acceptable at all are not covered in the Official Rules of Golf. A golfer without his Official Rules of Golf is a golfer looking for a ruling. A golfer waiting for the acceptability of something not covered in the Official Rules of Golf is waiting to be not just ruled but dominated.

Within very narrow limits, I support the notion of gambling at golf. True gambling at golf is a wager on someone other than yourself. Who can say exactly how psychologically wiggly another golfer may be? His wardrobe and equipment may belie alarming psychic top-heaviness. To bet on another is akin to placing an overabundant confidence in the appearance of faith, hope, or charity. Certainly, these will all come—but don't bet on it.

How's that? Well, it's like betting on your hometown team. When the hometown team is very bad. It is quite enough to emotionally rise and fall and usually fail backing your own guys. We know the purity of disappointment that comes with backing the hometown loser. However, a hometown loser that has covered the spread is only a sister's kiss, a fish with feathers, or a donkey that wants to get to know you better.

The sum and substance of what I was hoping to express is this. In golf, just as in life—I hoped I could get that line in the book somewhere—the best wagers are laid on oneself. The second best are those laid on oneself and one's partner, at back-nine par-threes where you both get a stroke.

If you didn't have these moments, you'd quit. Not just because you can't break eighty, find time to practice, or lose the yips. Life just becomes complicated, and in order to do some things well, like parenting or spousing, certain things have to fall by the wayside. For me, it was hockey. No tears. No regrets. Hockey is out of my life now. Eliminating all televised sports is still on the docket. But, I've decided to keep and extend my golf time. Especially due to the time I spent golfing in Ireland. My favorite place to golf.

Guys immediately ask, "Can it be better than Pebble, or Augusta, or Pine Valley?" Most people who play these great American courses play them on a pass, and it's palpable as you play—I am a guest here. Imagine playing an equally beautiful, equally challenging course, and being treated like a king. That is the Irish experience. There the nineteenth hole is mandatory, as are twenty and twenty-one.

The hospitality is possibly genetic, or tribal; all my ancestors are Irish. My first visit I was recognized—"John Belushi!"—and introduced to John Power's "the whiskey in the wood," served from its barrel on the back bar. Hours later these Dubliners had invited me back home, treated me to an impromptu concert of guitar, tin whistle, fiddle, and mandolin. I, for my part, sat bedazzled on the hardwood floor from where I began lecturing the lads on how I would reunite the counties and bring an end to the strife between North and South.

I was "made aware" with the first notes of recorded music heard that evening. A record player came alive with the strains of a traditional song called "Johnny Jump Up."

> Oh, never, oh, never, oh, never again,
> If I live to be a hundred,
> Or a hundred and ten,
> For I fell on the floor,
> And I could not get up;
> After drinking a quart
> Of old Johnny Jump Up."

As the agents say—two things—1) Jimmy Crowley does it on his album *Uncorked*, and 2) I was the one on the floor, full of Johnny Jump Up. I got it very quickly that the song was meant for more than entertainment and asked, "Might that be me that you're referring to?"

And they answered just as quickly, "Yes, you're correct: and it's quite all right."

Drunk on the floor, telling them how to run their own country, and it's quite all right. In that case, I made an internal pledge, I'm just gonna make plans to come back real soon and stay longer next time.

That 'tis a lovely emerald isle is a bit of an understatement. There are so many greens, you could almost think that green is the new brown, and brown the new black. The late Michael Kelly of Chicago remarked that Dublin reminded him of Indianapolis. You'd jump from the grave, Kelly, to see Dublin now. Once empty squares . . . now a sea of youth that formerly expatriated to make a living. The gripe used to be that the food wasn't too good. The four basics—bread, butter, milk, and bacon— were excellent, even better than here in the States. With Guinness as backup, one could easily survive. And since my first visit, the influence of nouvelle cuisine has risen—and with that the nation's food slope rating.

And by the way, has anyone thought to blame the English invaders for the bad food? Don't ever forget the plastic bullets, but don't forget the pernicious British diet, either.

My brothers and I returned to the ould sod to do a comedy festival in Kilkenny. We went with other graduates of Chicago's Second City theater to perform some old chestnuts created on Wells Street twenty years ago. Our one review said our material wasn't as cutting edge as some of the standup comedians. Next time . . . fifteen-year-old material.

Doing old material isn't my idea of a great time. And my brothers Joel and Brian could care as little for the punt as the dollar, but at the offer of a golf tour after the festival, we bit. The cast rehearsed at my home for a week, then we flew to Shannon where we were ensconced at Gutralogah House, a lovely manor on Lough Derg near Nenagh in County Tipperary. The weather was soft and foggy, making the hikes on the lake and in the woods quite dreamy. The nighttime sleep was excellent by necessity, the work forcing us to forgo our daily naps. Every meal was outstanding.

The piano was in the parlor, so we took that room over for the week. Our last night we did the show for our host, their neighbors, and friends. We made our entrances and exits from closets, stairwells, and behind draperies. I'm proud to say for as good as we got, we gave. We settled up in international currency—the magic of theater.

There was a man, one sent from God, whose name was Sean. He was not himself the Light, but came to bear witness concerning the Kilkenny Golf Club as its secretary and General Manager.

Sean O'Neill was our man's name. I don't remember how or where we met him, but once we did, we were made men. He knew pubs that weren't jammed with the Festival crowds (including a few with a secret), a couple of decent places to eat, but mostly he was our golf man. We were the guests.

So each night we had a show time. At six P.M., and at the club by eight, and the blessing of the summer's northern sky enabled us to play until ten-thirty. The light was so beautiful and the sky was so lovely.

O'Neill could play, too. He was perhaps sixty, reminiscent of a Pat O'Brien, but he won every match we played with him. He always figures a way to make par. He was intrigued by our golf tour to come and must have asked me our schedule fifteen or twenty times. And each time I'd complete the itinerary he'd remark, "Bill, if you get the chance, you must play Waterville. You really must play Waterville." Pronounced "Wot-ur-vul."

We comped his tickets every night of the show, and all his friends and most of his relations saw us. And after at the pub, waiting for the pints to settle, he'd turn to me and say, "Bill, if you get the chance, you must play Wot-ur-vul. My friend Neil Cronin is the secretary down there. I'll talk to him and see if he can arrange it."

Our plans took us from Mt. Juliet near Kilkenny, out to the west to Dingle, the Ballybunion, then Dooks. Dooks would be as close as we'd get to Wot-ur-vul. Each time I told him our plan, I'd finish with Dooks, and he'd repeat it. "Dooks? If you get the chance, you must play

Wot-ur-vul. My friend Neil Cronin is the secretary down there."

He came to see us off, his face miles away as I thanked him for his kindness. Finally he looked at me and said, "If you teed off at Dooks—played one, two, three, five, eight, nine, seventeen, and eighteen—you could still make it down to Wot-ur-vul in time for a full eighteen. If you get the chance, you must play . . ." The rest was drowned out by the engine of our lorry as it pulled away. I wonder what he said.

The locals disparage Mt. Juliet as a golf course "too American." Jack Nicklaus designed it on property owned by the Butler family. I guess it is manicured by Irish standards, but it is gorgeous. I have never seen a four-hundred-year-old chestnut tree, and one fairway has three of them. I have a beautiful copper beech at my home; Mt. Juliet has over a dozen of them in a row. Ridiculous. And the hospitality and attention is absurd by normal standards.

You can flag down any employee, headed anywhere on the property, and ask for anything:

"I have a golf shoe back in my room that is missing a Softspike."

"We better go back there, have a look, see if we can fix it."

Andrew Whitacre is the perfect caddy: scratch handicap, former psychology major, and no outstanding warrants.

And around he or she would swing, and ferry you back to where you needed mending. I hated leaving.

Dingle is not an overpowering golf course, but the where there is beyond compare. The peninsula and the mountains of Sleigh Head, where David Lean shot *Ryan's Daughter*. You can only call it laughingly beautiful. You just keep turning—turning to see this vista, then that vista, walking the course, turning around in its beauty until you're drunk.

Ballybunion is a great Irish joke, a song sung outdoors, and a beautiful woman sleepin' on your shoulder. Enough?

And Dooks must have been built by the Celts after a season of beheading Vikings. It's primitive, savage, cruel, black Irish mischief. That's a thumbnail sketch, because we only played one, two, three, five, eight, nine, seventeen, and eighteen.

The weather got wild as we followed our whiskey route. Huge wind, black sky, a hole called The Bowl, where only one landing spot held the green. And the eighteenth green protected an earth wall with only a keyhole to shoot through, but we were ready, and we had the chance. We knew we must play Waterville. The road to Waterville wasn't crowded that day. All the goats were napping, I guess. Treacherous, washed out, wave after

I was practicing at the far end of the Grand Cypress range one morning. There wasn't another soul there, just a set of clubs in one of the stands a few yards from me. Then a figure appeared in the distance. He was on a bicycle, at the same time carrying a boom box. It was Bill. He gave me a quick nod, then walked to the clubs, set down his box, and flipped on a tape. It was an out-there rock group called Big Head Todd and the Monsters. He hit balls to the music for a while, then picked up the box, nodded goodbye, and pedaled off.

—*Cheryl Anderson,*
LPGA Teaching Professional

wave of blinding water. Death awaited us at every turn. I was Sandra Bullock in *Speed 2*.

We arrived in the midst of a general evacuation of the clubhouse parking lot. We tried to act as casually as we could in what can only be described as Weather Channel highlights. The uprise was that Neil Cronin was expecting us.

We teed off at 6:15 P.M. in a thirty-five-mile-an-hour gale. You could see a four-iron's distance.

"Where is the green?"

"It's out there."

The rain really did come sideways. God, it was fun. I felt like the bishop in *Caddyshack,* played by Henry Wilcoxon. And like him, playing too well to stop. And besides, I didn't think the heavy stuff was going to come down for quite some time.

When Henry and I shot that scene, it was underneath rain-machine whirlybirds that provided five times the amount of water as normal rainfall, so that it would read on camera. We were drowned like rats after one take, but we enjoyed it so much, we kept doing it until we reached the delirium you see in the film. Henry was seventy-five then, and it was his last big role. When he arrived in America from the U.K. in the thirties, he was a major stud. He was the original Marc Antony to Claudette Colbert's Cleopatra. Check him out on AMC Classics. He was a real man. Fearlessly kind.

Where was I. Oh, yeah, wet. At the turn, we re-entered the clubhouse to a few folks who thought we were stopping. No, we just didn't have on the right clothes.

They called the manager of the pro shop at home. He came back to the club, and we outfitted the entire group, caddy included, in proper halibut-fishing attire. The real stuff is not cheap, poor people must get very, very wet on days like this. It was a good thing we did, though, because the weather got bad.

They knew we were men now, except for Megan Fay, our enchanting forty-one-inch blonde good luck charm. We brought her along 'cause she had a good short game. And just in case the Legend of the White Walrus was true.

We didn't talk much, we wouldn't have heard. But our faces said that we were alive, very alive, hitting drivers from elevated par threes that came up short, inspiring a caddy to be as loyal as a setter, but not so skittish.

You wanted it to never end, but finally there was a building in the gloamin', and out to the eighteenth green raced a barman, and crouched next to him another guy held an umbrella over them and their treasure—glasses fully charged with Black Bush.

"Git tunder here!" he roared from beneath the brolly. It may have been the daffiest thing I've ever heard. I am a human galosh after hours in a directionless gale, and he thinks to cover me bonnet. Ta.

We sat in front of the peat fire for quite some time with the owner of the course, an American called Jay Connolly. I caught him staring a couple of times. He asked for our scorecards and a blood sample, and said if we ever returned he wanted plenty of notice.

My head and brain seemed very large, yet quiet inside. The same feeling at the end of the *Hamlet* scene which closed our show. It was set in limbo where the characters of the play arrived, one by one, to wait for their deaths to be avenged. When Hamlet finally arrives and his father demands vengeance, Hamlet says "No, N,A,Y, no. You asked me to avenge you and look what happened. I killed Polonius, I killed Laertes, I killed Claudius, I was responsible for Ophelia's death. You say you won't be happy till your death is avenged . . ." And then a Clark Gable "Well frankly, father, I don't give a damn." Followed by a madrigal, penned by Fred Kaz, the musical genius of Second City:

When you were alive, you used to fight about your
   death

Now that you're dead, you ought to take a look
   around
Not such an awful place to be, to be, to be.
Back when getting even meant a man against a man
When codes of honor justified a homicide
Why didn't some guy cry "No more, no more, no
   more,"
Then this might have been the final score, now war
To be, to be, sure beat the shit out of not to be.
To be.

Some nights in Kilkenny there wasn't a dry eye in the place.

And now every time I drink Bushmills, I think, "Shouldn't I be wetter?"